KT-432-408

# WRINKLIES'
# WIT & WISDOM
## RIDES AGAIN

First published in Great Britain in 2008 by Prion
an imprint of the
Carlton Publishing Group
20 Mortimer Street
London W1T 3JW

2 4 6 8 10 9 7 5 3 1

Text copyright © Allison Vale and Alison Rattle
Design and layout copyright © Carlton Publishing Group

The right of Allison Vale and Alison Rattle to be identified as the
authors of this work has been asserted by them in accordance with
the Copyright, Designs and Patents Act 1988. All rights reserved. This
book is sold subject to the condition that it may not be reproduced,
stored in a retrieval system or transmitted in any form or by means,
electronic, mechanical, photocopying, recording or otherwise,
without the publisher's prior consent.

A catalogue record for this book is available from the British Library

ISBN 978-1-85375-658-0

Typeset by E-type, Liverpool

Printed in Great Britain

# WRINKLIES' WIT & WISDOM
## RIDES AGAIN

*Alison Rattle & Allison Vale*

PRION

# CONTENTS

# Introduction

The structure of the population of Great Britain is undergoing a significant change. Recent studies have shown that over the next 25 years the number of people over the age of 50 will increase by 6 million, whilst the number of people between the ages of 16-50 will decrease by 1.5 million. Already more than 80% of the nation's wealth is controlled by the over 45s. Grandmothers are more likely to be seen flashing their cash in the shopping centre on a Saturday than their granddaughters, and the over 50s now spend more money on the latest music releases than teenagers.

In previous generations, a man in his mid-sixties was old, looking forward to nothing more exciting than a permanent residence in his favourite armchair. A woman of the same age was overlooked and invisible, settling quietly for a well-worn dotage, her once celebrated good looks nothing more than a dim memory. The image and expectations of elderly people have changed dramatically in recent times. Today's wrinklies are not interested in longevity so much as the *quality* of life they are leading. The upcoming older generation are far more likely to invest their money in having a good time *now*, than to think about retirement and pensions, and slowing down. They are not interested in growing old.

# Introduction

Today's 50-plus generation can reminisce about their wild youth like no generation before: theirs was a purple haze of sex, drugs, and rock and roll. And they still thrive on excitement; they have lost neither their verve nor vigour. They are as addicted to sensation-seeking decadence as ever they were in their youth. No surprise that they are widely celebrated in the media as the "young old".

The cult of celebrity fuels this trend. Mick Jagger still rocks stadiums at 63, strutting his trim 28-inch waist, so they say, for an average of 12 miles every time he puts on a show. Cilla, sent reeling at first by widowhood, has recovered to embrace her "sexties" with gusto. Joan Collins, married to a man 31 years her junior, brushes off the age gap like a true diva: "If he dies, he dies."

These rocking wrinklies champion causes like never before, too, challenging our youth-led culture to face up to the short-comings of our society and inspiring a healthy political activism in us all. Bono and Geldof may have pioneered the celebrity charitable cause in the '80s, but legions of others have since made it their own. Big names from the music industry, and from the stage and screen, are prepared time and again to campaign for causes they care about: Paul Weller, Jane Fonda, Ben Elton, Helen Mirren, Ted Danson, to name but a few.

High expectations for a decadent dotage are not the sole reserve of the rich and famous, but are widely embraced by baby boomers everywhere. Women in their 60s are having babies and starting new careers, while men in their 90s are exploring the North Pole. Grandparents are now spending more money than ever before on their grandchildren. Not just on material gifts, but on going to new places and experiencing new things. Whilst the grandchildren are begging to sit down and rest at the theme park, Grannie and

# Introduction

Grandpa are first in the queue for the sensational new roller coaster ride.

The gap between old and young is decreasing rapidly and manufacturers of goods aimed at the older generation are having to re-think how they market their products. The fashion industry has experienced the biggest change, with older folk now eschewing the traditional 'fuddy duddy' outlets and choosing to shop instead at the same stores as their children and grandchildren. Manufacturers of goods which relate specifically to the ageing process are having to be very clever with their advertising. People no longer want bi-focals, but are happy to accept 'progressive lenses', and the makers of stair lifts can no longer use the traditional image of a granny and her knitting needles being transported slowly up the stairs. A stair lift with racing stripes and a passenger plugged into an iPod is far more likely to sell.

In the '60s the baby boomers reinvented what it was to be young. They proved that activism could influence government policy; they yearned for a different lifestyle and fought hard to earn it; they refused to lower their expectations. And throughout it all, they made time to party. Now in their 50s and 60s, the same generation are not about to break the habits of a lifetime. They are no more able or likely to shrink into quiet, unassuming decrepitude in their senior years as they were in their youth. Older celebrities who look wonderful for their age have become role models, proving unequivocally that you can be suave, stunning and sexy at any age. Today's older generation have followed suit (and if they need a bit of pulling or tweaking to get there… well they can afford it!)

Rocking wrinklies are just as fully engaged with life as they have ever been, fuelled by their passions, pumped up by their own potential and looking great.

# A Wild Youth

I looked upon myself, in a sort of romantic and silly way, as like a laboratory.

> *Keith Richards, talking about his wild, drug-taking youth*

Eddy: You know, Patsy used to date Keith Moon.
Patsy: Well, sort of. I woke up underneath him in a hotel room once.

> Absolutely Fabulous

I never said I was the Virgin Mary. It is dangerous to be considered perfect.

> *Catherine Deneuve reflecting on her episodes of tax-avoidance*

When I was on drugs I couldn't write, I couldn't perform. Drugs take away any ambition. Now I'm not ambitious – not for any chemical reason, but because I've got what I want.

> *Marianne Faithful*

I'm four and a half years clean and sober, so the energy's starting to come back.

> *Elton John*

# A Wild Youth

I knew I had to change. I was either going to die or change. I thought, what have I come to? I'm either going to carry on like I am and die of a heart attack or an OD, or I'm going to get my life together.

*Elton John*

I nearly killed all the Pythons. My mother had lent me her Dormobile van and I was driving everyone back home after a night out. It was a bit foggy and this was before any modern wisdom about drink-driving. It was only when we were overtaken by another car, going in the same direction as us but on the other side of the divide, that I realised we'd been going the wrong way up the motorway.

*Douglas Adams*

People expect a bit of outrage [from celebrities] and they don't mind all that much if you keel over in the corner of the room or something.

*Graham Chapman*

Those bloody stomach throws! They used to give me bigger and better men every time. That's one reason why my back isn't so good, because I was always rolling on the base of my spine. I must have been mad.

*Honor Blackman*

Saffy (to Patsy): Why aren't you dead?
Edina: Darling… because she started young. When

other kids were playing pin the donkey, Patsy was lookin' for a vein.

Absolutely Fabulous

I'm sure some 'sexpert' would now class my womanising as a 'compulisve sex disorder' and pack me off to an expensive corrective facility. But I refuse to feel guilty about my behaviour back then.

*Tony Blackburn*

I suppose it's just a bit of a shame that, while others of my generation were taking drugs or dancing or having wild sex, I was doodling drawings of Scania tractor units.

*Alexi Sayle*

As a teenager I was the average aspirant yob. I wanted to be menacing, but I was brought up in Cheam – and rebelling in Cheam means going through the traffic lights when they're on amber.

*Jeremy Vine*

Who cares? Let's get it out there, while it lasts. At 70, I'll be throwing them over my shoulders. They'll become a wrap – put some fox fur on the ends, or something.

*Catherine Zeta Jones referring to her topless photos*

I became very famous, as a teenager, and my name and photo were splashed in all the media. They made me larger than life, so I wanted to live larger than life and the only way to do that was to be intoxicated.

*Cat Stevens*

## Put Out to Pasture

I had no idea what the effect would be of walking out of
a relationship with the man I loved – and God I loved
Mick [Jagger], still do – and choosing to live in St Anne's
Court [Soho], shooting up heroin, plagued by anorexia.

*Marianne Faithful*

## Put Out to Pasture

People started to tell me that I wasn't young
anymore early on in my career. When, at 25, I told
a Hollywood producer my age, he informed me
cynically, "Twenty-five? Honey, that's not young in this
town anymore."

*Joan Collins,* The Art of Living Well

Television is showing that the audience is there for
dramas that depict more complicated women – and by
complicated, I mean anyone over 25.

*Laura Bickford, movie producer*

There is this group of wonderful actresses – Mirren,
Streep, Redgrave, Bening and Christie, to name just a
few – who don't stop being great just because they've
reached a certain age. In fact, their performances are
even richer because of their age and experience.

*Daniel Battsek, head of Miramax*

There are fewer roles, but the roles get better as you
get older. They become deeper, more complicated

and more interesting. It's those young roles that are tedious.

*Helen Mirren*

Love stories about older people tend to be either extremely sentimentalised or justified by a million flashbacks to when they were young, which I think is a lot less interesting.

*Sarah Polley, actor, director and screenwriter*

I think attitudes [towards older women] are exactly where they were, particularly where women are concerned. When women of 60-something can get jobs and are seen on television then I will believe attitudes to ageing are changing.

*Michele D'Argy Smith, former editor of* Cosmopolitan

The media would have us believe that ageing is harder for women, which might be true, but then, hey, men age too. For example, how hairy are my toes becoming?

*Jeff Green*

Girls have a harder time with longevity, since so many of them are hired for being fresh and pretty.

*Steve Martin, discussing women's careers in the movie industry*

I think there is a growing acceptance of the fact that women actually make up 50% of the population. And that women of our generation are an economic force.

*Helen Mirren on women's roles in film*

# Put Out to Pasture

We're in such a youth-driven society. It's fine to be youthful and vibrant and try to look good, but do it in a realistic way. Don't set yourself up for failure – set yourself up for joy. Why try to be someone you're not? You might as well try to be the real thing.

*Cheryl Ladd*

Funny business, a woman's career. The things you drop on the way up the ladder so you can move faster. You forget you'll need them again when you get back to being a woman.

*Bette Davis,* All About Eve

It's a narrower field as you get older and there are roles that come along, and some of them are just not that good, so what's the point you know?

*Goldie Hawn*

TV has gone back to the '50s in its attitude to female presenters. They just want a pretty face.

*Ruby Wax*

When you get to a certain age, the work begins to thin out.

*Charles Dance*

There was a long time that I wanted to have blonde hair, be called Tracey and go out with boys.

*Meera Syal*

# Put Out to Pasture

The brutal truth of television is that they don't employ old people or fat people.

*Ruby Wax*

I'd had a career playing mostly romantic leading men and there is an optimum age for those characters – around 40, tops.

*Charles Dance*

As I sat around with friends, I'd think, "…yes, your hair is greying and some bits are sagging, but you're more beautiful than ever and you've got so many fascinating stories to tell." I'm hacked off that we're not seeing that reflected on our screens.

*Meera Syal*

I'm not dead. I mean, I may be getting older, but I'm not dead!

*Sheryl Crow*

When I was 49 I posed for *Playboy* – I was very flattered to be asked. I was quite honoured really, considering that most of the models they feature are in their 20s.

*Joan Collins*

And probably in the back of my mind, like most women, I didn't really want to think that I was starting to go into menopause. At that point, it wasn't something that I was embracing. Especially in my industry, getting older is a big no-no; as if we have any choice.

*Cheryl Ladd*

## Youngsters Today

Like all old people, [I] despise young people, with their
bendy bodies and their hangovers that last a millisecond.

*Jeff Green*

I find the attitude of certain young people – i.e., that
being young is to be a superior being – rather pathetic,
and certainly short-sighted…

*Joan Collins,* The Art of Living Well

The dead might as well try to speak to the living as the
old to the young.

*Willa Cather*

When you're 18 you think everyone over 40 plays
dominoes and smells of Vick.

*Jasper Carrott*

That's the thing about getting older, the young are
getting weirder.

*Jenny Hjul,* The Scotsman

A hundred things are done today in the divine name of
Youth that if they showed their true colors would be
seen by rights to belong rather to old age.

*Wyndham Lewis*

A young boy is a theory; an old man is a fact.

*Edgar Watson Howe*

Get to my age and they treat you as though you're
educationally subnormal. And deaf – they always shout at
you. And I'm not deaf. Or daft... The trouble is, you get
used to it. You do! You begin to believe that you are past it.
You start acting like a child because you're expected to,
and before you know it, you've given up. I've still got a
brain – what's left of it – and I still have opinions, but they
don't seem to count anymore. Who cares what I think?

Rosie, *by Alan Titchmarsh*

There is something at the back of one's mind telling
one that we have had it very easy and that we have not
been sufficiently appreciative of our parents's
generation, who didn't have it very easy.

*Jeremy Paxman*

The worst thing you can do with young people is say,
"Yeah when I was your age... " because they just hate
you instantly for saying that. You were never their age;
their age is unique; they are the first people to ever have
been young, and the experience they are going through
is unique... much more profound and resonant than
anything you could have gone through, so never ever
try to connect with young people.

*Kathryn Flett,* Grumpy Old Women

Teenagers travel in droves, packs, swarms. To the librarian,
they're a gaggle of geese. To the cook, they're a scourge of
locusts. To department stores, they're a big beautiful
exaltation of larks. All lovely and loose and jingly.

*Bernice Fitz-Gibbon*

# Youngsters Today

My research team tells me young people do not read newspapers these days, being either too busy downloading ring tones for their telephones, or too morbidly obese to make it to the newsagents.

*Martin Kelner,* The Guardian

Youth is when you're allowed to stay up late on New Year's Eve. Middle age is when you're forced to.

*Bill Vaughn*

In youth the days are short and the years are long. In old age the years are short and day's long.

*Pope Paul VI*

Our grandfathers had to run, run, run. My generation's out of breath. We ain't running no more.

*Stokely Carmichael*

Parents who wonder where the younger generation is going should remember where it came from.

*Sam Ewing*

They say that we are better educated than our parents' generation. What they mean is that we go to school longer. They are not the same thing.

*Douglas Yates*

The best thing to do is just treat young people as an alien species, what is what they are, and between the ages of about 12, 13, to 20, 21, just ignore them.

*Kathryn Flett,* Grumpy Old Women

# The Thing About Old People

I wouldn't be young again even if it were possible.

*Ruth Rendell*

There's a lot to do when you're a kid – spiders to catch, girls to poke in the eye – stuff to be getting on with.

*Alan Davies*

I wouldn't want to be in my 20s again – not even if you could give that time back to me tomorrow.

*Kim Basinger*

I don't mind being old. What I do mind is when the younger ones have no respect and treat you as if you were stupid.

*Nadine Richardson, 70, member of rock band, The Zimmers*

# The Thing About Old People

Nobody really talks to old people, cos, you know, you don't know what they're saying. They just go, "arghh, arghh, arghh," and you don't know if they're having a good time or being bitten.

*Dylan Moran*

Grannies drink all the time, don't they? All afternoon, just pints of lager. Every time I'd go round, she'd be like this, "Let's have a little sherry". I'd be like, "Why?" She'd be like, "Because I'm old."

*Rhona Cameron*

# The Thing About Old People

My dad is really just a series of sound effects now.

*Maria Bamford*

My Dad. I met him off the train once. I said, "Hello
Dad, how was your train journey?"
He said, "You ever been on a train?"
"Yeah"
"It was like that."
Charming.

*Jeff Green*

[Older comedians] will never admit to ever having
done or said anything wrong, ever, in their working
lives. It is always somebody else's fault when their career
takes a downturn. It is the fault of the pregnant
showgirl, or the slimy, liberal (probably Jewish)
documentary makers who secretly filmed them telling
racist jokes to a howling audience of policemen, or the
upcoming generation of alternative (probably Jewish)
po-faced comedians who don't know what's funny.

*Alexi Sayle*

In about 40 years, we'll have thousands of old ladies
running around with tattoos.

*Anon*

Old men are like that, you know. It makes them feel
important to think they are in love with somebody.

*Willa Cather*

Old women with mobile phones look wrong!

*Peter Kay*

# The Thing About Old People

Call this an unfair generalization if you must, but old people are no good at everything.

*Moe, from* The Simpsons

The problem with me is, I guess, the way I express myself, you have to be with me 50 years before you can get a sense of what I'm talking about.

*Al Pacino*

I'm just an old man and I smell bad, remember?

*Stanley Kubrick*

Inside many of us is a small old man who wants to get out.

*Anne Sexton*

Maturity is often more absurd than youth and very frequently is most unjust to youth.

*Thomas A Edison*

Only the middle-aged have all their five senses in the keeping of their wits.

*Hervey Allen*

All I'm saying is that old people need to be old people. You need oldness. You need to see old people. You need to go "Right, they might have a solution, they've been on the earth longer. Quick, we need an answer".

*Karl Pilkington —Podcast Series 3, Episode Four*

The closing years of life are like the end of a masquerade party, when the masks are dropped.

*Arthur Schopenhauer*

# Politically Active Seniors

Have you not a moist eye, a dry hand, a yellow cheek, a white beard, a decreasing leg, an increasing belly? Is not your voice broken, your wind short, your chin double, your wit single, and every part about you blasted with antiquity?

*J B Priestley*

Getting older isn't the same as it was. When Paul McCartney sang "When I'm 64," being 64 was in your dotage. It's not now.

*Paul Merton*

The sight of an old woman [Joan Collins] still apparently believing that self-esteem depends on looking good and having a man is profoundly depressing, not to mention exhausting.

*Frances Taylor,* The Times

Age can bring people independence of thought. Older people are not afraid to be original. They have the confidence to be off-message.

*Dr David Olivier, expert in ageing*

# Politically Active Seniors

Worrying about whether or not you lose work for speaking out is like worrying about your slip showing when you're fleeing a burning building. At the end of the day you have to be able to say to your kids: "I asked questions. I tried." Otherwise you can't live with yourself.

*Susan Sarandon*

The Aids emergency is just that. It's not a cause…
Several thousand people dying a day is not a cause, it's
an emergency.

*Bono*

You want to talk about poverty alleviation? Don't
show me any more bloody plastic bangles. Show me
you can trade in epicentres of absolute economic
despair, sit with marginalised people, buy ingredients
from them.

*Anita Roddick*

Democracy is a device that insures we shall be governed
no better than we deserve.

*George Bernard Shaw*

I'm fond of Tony Blair and Gordon Brown. They are
kind of the John and Paul of the global development
stage, in my opinion. But the point is, Lennon and
McCartney changed my interior world – Blair and
Brown can change the real world.

*Bono*

The truth is, I came out of the womb an activist and I
will go to the grave an activist.

*Anita Roddick*

I'm really sorry for Tony Blair. He pushed this to the
point of exhaustion so well done him, he had nothing
to lose so he went out all guns blazing.

*Bob Geldof, referring to Blair's efforts in the G8*

# Politically Active Seniors

Africa makes a fool of our idea of justice; it makes a
farce of our idea of equality. It mocks our pieties, it
doubts our concern, it questions our commitment.

*Bono*

It makes me mad to see this guy [US Vice President
Dick Cheney] standing up there saying we're not ready
[for energy conservation in the US]. We were ready 20
years ago for alternatives. The oil company lobbies are
just too big!

*Jane Fonda*

You see, deep down, if we really accepted that Africans
were equal to us, we would all do more to put the fire
out. We've got watering cans, when what we really need
are the fire brigades.

*Bono, addressing a Labour Party Conference in 2004*

I was the first woman to burn a bra… it took the fire
department four days to put it out.

*Dolly Parton*

If we come out of the G8 having achieved something
for the weakest, voiceless, most put-upon people in the
planet, that would not be a bad use of political
influence.

*Bob Geldof*

Run for office? No. I've slept with too many women, I've
done too many drugs and I've been to too many parties.

*George Clooney*

Individuals are not powerless; we don't have to rely on governments. One goat costs just £12: you don't have to do big things to make a difference.

*Patricia Parker, who founded the charity, 'Kids for Kids' at the age of 51, supplying families with goats in the Sudan*

Government's view of the economy could be summed up in a few short phrases. If it moves, tax it. If it keeps moving, regulate it. And if it stops moving, subsidise it.

*Ronald Reagan*

Mick Jagger and I just really liked each other a lot. We talked all night. We had the same views on nuclear disarmament.

*Jerry Hall*

The subtext seems to be that it's a second–class option not to have a father. He may feel that, and he's perfectly entitled to his opinion, but society has changed, fundamentally. He can't turn the clock back. The nuclear family is no longer the absolute way. He's just got to accept that.

*Ben Elton, talking about Australian PM John Howard's views on IVF for lesbian couples*

I've talked to you on a number of occasions about the economic problems our nation faces, and I am prepared to tell you it's in a hell of a mess – we're not connected to the press room yet, are we?

*Ronald Reagan*

# Politically Active Seniors

I don't think I'm any more outspoken than any old pub bore, going on about what's wrong with the government. I just have a wider pub. But I'm still connected with my society, and I'll say what I think when I feel like it.

*Ben Elton*

I had to go back to Ireland to bury my grandmother last summer and it was bizarre… not least because it was a military funeral, because my grandmother fought in the Irish War of Independence, against yourselves about 80 years or so ago, right? And it was bizarre because she's my granny. To me she's a small woman, you know: stooped; lucozade; crisps. Used to give me a selection box at Christmas and a birthday card with a tenner in it, right, every year. That's me granny. No. There were six blokes with guns standing over her grave, firing shots… and I'm sitting there, going, "I didn't really know her at all. This woman had hidden depths which I was unaware of." (And just so as you know, it was an official Irish military funeral … they weren't wearing balaclavas. They didn't disappear into the crowd after they'd fired the shots, right?)

*Dara O' Briain*

Politicians are a lot like diapers. They should be changed frequently and for the same reasons.

*Robin Williams*

I'm for total honest democracy. I also believe the American system can work.

*Woody Allen,* Stardust Memories

# Politically Active Seniors

Governments change, the lies stay the same.

*Pierce Brosnan,* Golden Eye

How could I look my grandchildren in the eye and say I knew about this – and I did nothing?

*David Attenborough, on climate change*

I view Tony Blair as, kind of, the air-guitarist of political rhetoric.

*Will Self*

They are absolutely killing us, but I am determined not to give in and have our food chain owned by a few multi-national companies. Farmers are like priests. Destroy those people and we will never get them back.

*Roger Daltrey on small farms*

You read about the state of the world and what's going on, and what our part in creating chaos becomes, and it's disturbing.

*Samuel L Jackson*

One of the problems with oceans is one half of one per cent of all the money that goes into environmental causes goes to marine work. All the rest, 99% of it, goes to land-based organizations.

*Ted Danson*

As you get older, the world starts to change. I travel so much and people get talking… they don't like America so much anymore.

*Samuel L Jackson*

# Politically Active Seniors

There's always so many despicable things in the world happening, but I just thought that was particularly shocking. I don't know how much lower we can ----ing get as a human race. These people aren't freedom fighters, they're just cowards.

*Paul Weller, referring to the Beslan school massacre*

Do you do this with Christmas tree lights? You have a string of them and one bulb is dead, and you flick the bulb with your finger to get it to light up? Same thing they do with George Bush before a debate.

*Jay Leno*

Meanwhile, hospitals aren't getting any better. I don't know where all our taxes go to – it certainly isn't into any welfare system or schools. All my kids have to go to private school to get a decent education. They can find the money to go to war, though – imagine how many millions a day that is. It's a phony veneer of democracy.

*Paul Weller*

The great challenge is to make people realise the power they have to change the world. It can be changed, you know. This Trident is wicked.

*Eileen Daffern, 93-year-old campaigner against nuclear weapons*

In the States, the election has become a so-called water cooler debate, meaning that Americans gather round the water cooler at work and discuss whether it would make a better president.

*Angus Deayton*

# Politically Active Seniors

Perhaps Ford, Land Rover's owners, might be doing the poor people of Darfur a favour if they continued selling Defenders to the Sudanese government, since if the feared janjaweed death squads were using Land Rovers they'd never get anywhere and would spend all the time they might have been ethnic cleansing instead hanging round the garage waiting for repairs or parts to be shipped from the UK.

*Alexi Sayle*

If there is one eternal truth about politics, it is that there are always a dozen good reasons for doing nothing.

*John le Carré*

It was the most difficult decision in my life – except the one in 1978 when I decided to get a bikini wax.

*Arnold Schwarzenegger, on his decision to run for Governor*

Now I am just an elderly lady who is full of spleen, who humps around greater Boston in a God-awful hat, who never lived and yet outlived her time hating men and dogs and Democrats.

*Anne Sexton*

Remember how he [Ronald Reagan] handled the Iran-contra Never Ending Scandal from Hell? He went on national television, the President of the United States, and said it wasn't his fault, because he was not aware, at the time, of what his foreign policy was.

*Dave Barry*

# Politically Active Seniors

Here's a man [Ronald Reagan] who was twice elected to the most powerful position on Earth despite needing a Teleprompter to correctly identify what year it was.

*Dave Barry*

Americans have different ways of saying things. They say "elevator", we say "lift" … they say "President" we say "tupid psychopathic git".

*Alexi Sayle*

One day, an army of grey-haired women may quietly take over the earth.

*Gloria Steinem*

Big business is already cashing in on the "silver pound". The fact is that more than 50% of the people who vote at the next General Election are likely to be over 50. That's real power. And political parties which do not understand that those over 50 have particular interests and needs, that must be addressed, will suffer the consequences.

*Menzies Cambell*

I have one simple principle in foreign affairs. I look at what the Americans are doing and then do the opposite. That way I can be sure I'm right.

*President Jacques Chirac*

I can't believe that this woman [Laura Bush] is as stupid as she pretends to be… We have a first lady who goes to

Africa and tells the people "to practice abstinence", that "Aids is an affliction". Honey please.

*Sandra Bernhard*

An Englishman can be defined as someone who lives on an island in the North Sea governed by Scots.

*Jeremy Paxman*

The problem is that many MPs never see the London that exists beyond the wine bars and brothels of Westminster.

*Ken Livingstone*

It's changed my life in a big way to see how unimportant what I do really is compared with the challenges that face them and their families. To see their courage and dignity is amazing, and very inspirational.

*Sue Barker, about her charity work for muscular dystrophy*

It's so hard to get how anything can be wrong with the oceans. Look how vast and beautiful they are. So that, and *Cheers* paying me silly amounts of money, made me start to think more seriously about what I should be doing.

*Ted Danson*

Our aim this year is to do something for England. So we are getting behind the Teenage Cancer Trust and aim to build at least one new ward.

*Roger Daltrey*

# Modern Warfare

You have to put your money where your mouth is – if you like all this. It all depends on oil. Either we decide to wean ourselves off oil, and we don't invade Iraq because we don't need to, or we stop being such hypocrites. People love what oil brings. The same people who are against the Iraq war are the same who insist on driving their children to school, because they can't contemplate that their child should walk.

*Helen Mirren*

The tragedy of modern war is that the young men die fighting each other – instead of their real enemies back home in the capitals.

*Edward Abbey*

In our name, the Bush administration… arrogated to itself and its allies the right to rain down military force anywhere and anytime. The brutal repercussions have been felt from the Philippines to Palestine… What kind of world will this become if the US government has a blank check to drop commandos, assassins and bombs wherever it wants?

*Jane Fonda*

I guess they all started getting a little worried when I wanted everyone in the Body Shop world to make a stand against the Iraqi invasion. It would have been suicide if we had done that in America.

*Anita Roddick*

The war against Iraq has unleashed unsuspected forces.
The first signs are twofold. The need of the Americans
to protect oil fields, but not hospitals, museums and
libraries. This is a catastrophic failure of imagination…
It does not bode well for the future.

*Ben Okri*

I was angry with Blair for the decision to go to war
[with Iraq].

*Robert Lindsay*

I performed at an anti-Iraq-war gig before the 2003
invasion and I'm disgusted at our role in the
continuation of the mess in the Middle East.

*Paul Weller*

Though times have changed, it's a nice surprise to see
that youthful feeling of anti-war sentiment returning
once more to the cobbled main streets of Europe.

*Cat Stevens*

## Royalty

Ageing did not come into it. I didn't mind that. But to
play a living monarch? And a monarch who enjoys
love and respect after 55 years on the throne? That was
a tall order, particularly as I was playing her at a point
when she was getting it wrong directly after Princess
Diana's death.

*Helen Mirren, on her nervousness at the prospect
of playing the Queen*

# Royalty

I was overcome, the moment I walked through the door, with the need to steal something.

*Jeremy Clarkson, referring to being inside Buckingham Palace*

She had on just as much jewellery as I did, though maybe she was a little tastier with it.

*Dolly Parton, referring to meeting the Queen*

Tourists don't come for the food or the beaches, they come to London to shop, see the Queen and go to the theatre. Well, Ken Livingstone and his ilk have pretty well ruined the theatre, so that leaves only the shops and Her Majesty. Hurry though; it won't be long before the shops have gone.

*Tom Conti*

I vaguely remember the Coronation in 1953, and standing up at the end of movies for 'God Save the Queen'. No one walked out of the cinema, did they? Whether you believed in the structure of the monarchy was irrelevant, in a way.

*Helen Mirren*

I can hardly believe it but up there, in the palace, the Queen of England is expecting me.

*Rolf Harris, commenting on being asked by the Queen to paint her 80th birthday portrait*

The Duke and I were trading a lot of jokes, and both of them laughed out loud, which I was told is unusual. One of the butlers sidled up to me and said he is under orders to video *The Kumars* for the royals, so I assume they like it.

*Sanjeev Bhaskar, on his informal lunch at Buckingham Palace*

God save our gracious Queen: why would we invoke a non-specific deity to bail out these unelected spongers?

*Bill Bailey*

I once walked in on the Queen wearing her crown and pink, fluffy slippers.

*Paul Burrell*

I've spent a bit of time with the Prince of Wales, who I respect greatly. I'd give two cheers for the monarchy.

*Sting*

# Class, Equality and Ageism

His lordship may compel us to be equal upstairs, but there will never be equality in the servants' hall.

*James M Barrie*

Why do people always think the working classes can't have money or taste? Being working class isn't about that. It's about calling dinner 'tea' and forgetting to put your cup back on the saucer in a restaurant.

*Danny Baker*

# Class, Equality and Ageism

But British society has its own rigid hierarchies. They're just different. If you're called Wayne, or you say "serviette" instead of "napkin", it's unlikely you've got a title. There are all these little things that catch you out.

*Meera Syal*

I learned to change my accent; in England, your accent identifies you very strongly with a class, and I did not want to be held back.

*Sting*

People think there's a rigid class system here, but dukes have even been known to marry chorus girls. Some have even married Americans.

*Prince Philip*

Not only do we suffer from racism and sexism, but we also suffer from ageism. Once you reach a certain age you're not allowed to be adventurous, you're not allowed to be sexual, I mean is there a rule? Are you supposed to just die when you're 40?"

*Madonna*

One day, I opened "Eastern Eye" and I saw two headlines side by side. One read, "Asian women top the graduate league", and the other read, "Asian women top the suicide and self-harm league". I thought, "What's going on here? Why are we capable of creating so much and at the same time of destroying ourselves?"

*Meera Syal*

# Class, Equality and Ageism

We need to work harder to encourage young women to have not only the confidence, but also the imagination, to choose 'non-traditional' career paths.

*Diane Abbott, MP*

Too often the way we treat our elderly people is a matter of national shame. However, if you're in politics you can't take these things personally.

*Menzies Campbell*

The pleasure of writing as an Asian woman is the pleasure of exploding stereotypes.

*Meera Syal*

I came to Britain in 1960 and experienced a huge culture shock, because I expected everyone to treat me kindly and with respect, but Britain was cold, unwelcoming, violent and bleak.

*Floella Benjamin*

Your heart does sink sometimes when you open a script that you know is going to be predominantly Asian. You think, "What's it going to be this time, suicide bombers or arranged marriages?"

*Meera Syal*

In a way though I'm lucky – I can demonstrate on a daily basis just how unjustified age discrimination is, whereas there is no such opportunity for most of those treated unfairly in the workplace purely because of their age.

*Menzies Campbell*

# I'm a Celebrity

It's absolutely true that Menzies [Campbell] looks old. He looks about 86, not 66, but so what? People are living much longer and you can be a very good prime minister if you're much older than Menzies. I think it's a vile prejudice and I'm very sorry that the LibDems have given in to it.

*Andrew Gimson,* Daily Telegraph

# I'm a Celebrity

If I had to be honest, as I get older my desire for privacy intensifies. I make myself do things that keep me in the public eye, because that is the "law" of our times, a certain level of celebrity is necessary to even get your foot in the door.

*Toyah Wilcox*

Most idiots don't lose their privacy, they give it away.

*Chrissie Hynde*

I've never seen a reaction like it when Oprah walked on stage. If she ran for President she'd win, no doubt. It was as if a deity had walked on.

*Meera Syal*

But when I walk down the street, one out of a few hundred people will recognize me and that's how I want it. I want to buy a slice of pizza and sit on a step.

*Chrissie Hynde*

In Sainsbury's, people occasionally say, "Oh, I didn't think you'd be shopping here" – and it's like well, it's a supermarket. Where else am I supposed to get my food?

*Alison Steadman*

We're not a celebrity couple – we're not very good at all that. We're not the new Posh and Becks. We've never courted publicity, and we're not going to do *Hello!* Yesterday, I went into the local chippie. I've been going there for two and a half years, and yet the woman behind the counter still said, "Hello, mate. How's the mini-cab business going?"

*Sanjeev Bhaskar*

That's the trouble with being me. At this point, nobody gives a damn what my problem is. I could literally have a tumour on the side of my head and they'd be like, "Yeah, big deal. I'd eat a tumour every morning for the kinda money you're pulling down."

*Jim Carrey*

Marlene Dietrich invited me to hear her new record. We all went and gathered around the gramophone, and when we were settled the record was put on. It was simply an audience applauding her! We sat through the entire first side and then we listened to the other side: more of the same!

*Sir John Gielgud*

Yeah I love being famous. It's almost like being white.

*Chris Rock*

# I'm a Celebrity

I wasn't really into the stardom thing for myself. I never really did it. I'd stay in the background. In my book, there aren't any pictures of me with my arms round celebrities.

*David Gest*

It's such hard work, living in a fish bowl – so hard to make friends, to be the girl hanging off a rock star's arm.

*Marianne Faithful*

Well, it's always been that way… I have a little statuette of Nell Gwynn, who was Charles II's mistress. And she was an actress. They sold little china statuettes of her… I'm sure Eve had a following.

*Joan Rivers, discussing the cult of celebrity*

I was once approached by a man in a shop who said, "Here, you look just like that Andrew Marr… you poor bugger."

*Andrew Marr*

Being a celebrity hasn't made me more sympathetic to famous people. Most of them are whining little tossers.

*Piers Morgan.*

Isn't it a good feeling when you read the tabloids and realise that a lot of famous people are just as fucked up as you are?

*George Carlin*

# The Perks of Getting Older

The great thing about getting older is you don't give a damn. I don't care what I say. I speak my mind much more now than I used to. I'm much happier now.

*Anne Reid*

The great thing about getting older is that you learn that staying in is quite nice.

*Lenny Henry*

I would stand at the top of the stairs in the '70s and I'd think, "Ooh, about an hour to go: I'll be out of the studio and have a drink". And now I stand at the top of the stairs and I think, "This could end tomorrow," and it's a wonderful feeling, because then you really enjoy the moment…

*Michael Parkinson*

Maybe it will sound strange, but I look forward to being older, when looks become less of an issue and who you are is the point.

*Susan Sarandon*

It is one of the blessings of old friends that you can afford to be stupid with them.

*Ralph Waldo Emerson*

Today, I know myself. I know who I am.

*Catherine Deneuve*

# The Perks of Getting Older

There are so few perks about getting older. Everything heads south and you become less and less attractive, but one of the perks is that you can usually learn to come home to yourself. You're a little more comfortable in your skin, as saggy as it is. And that's a gift.

*Felicity Huffman* (Desperate Housewives)

I think age is a good thing, in the sense that it teaches you to reflect and take care of the past.

*Helen Mirren*

Getting older is a fascinating thing. The older you get, the older you want to get.

*Keith Richards*

I read a lot, I am on my own a lot. I'm better at being true to myself and only doing things I want to do.

*Marianne Faithful*

I'm more comfortable with being female now. I used to think I shouldn't wear make-up. I've had to learn how to walk in high heels. I have to shave my legs otherwise I'd look like a chimp… and I confess to loving a Brazilian!

*Emma Thompson*

There are things you can do in later life, such as developing a taste for claret. That is a rewarding hobby.

*Barbara Hoskins, press officer at 10 Downing Street under Harold Wilson and Edward Heath*

# The Perks of Getting Older

I enjoy my life, I've got lots of friends – and I don't do anything I don't want to. I think that's as good as it gets at 71.

*Joan Bakewell*

I've just been doing it [acting] for such a long time and the evidence builds up that you can kind of do it.

*Emma Thompson*

It is terrifying, because it takes much longer now [to learn my lines]. But you have to be careful not to let fear stop you doing things. It's very exciting to test yourself. I used to suffer from excessive pride – I'd be crippled if it wasn't immaculate. Well, I got over that one.

*Francesca Annis*

A few years ago, I was mostly concerned with getting things for myself – more clothes, more money, more popularity, more boyfriends. Then I woke up.

*Madonna*

It's just lovely getting older. You know, I don't worry so much about myself really. I feel as though now there is no time for any of that, there's no time to kvetch about who you are, what you mean. That sort of self-doubt belongs to when you're younger.

*Emma Thompson*

I never envy people looking younger. I wouldn't want to go back for anything. The pressures are huge.

*Jane Fonda*

# The Perks of Getting Older

For 25 years, I could never put a forkful in my mouth without feeling fear, without feeling scared. I'm 64 years old and only in the last two years have I learned that good enough is good enough.

*Jane Fonda*

I find I worry less about what people think of me… One takes things in one's stride more. I have a sense of freedom now.

*Elaine Paige*

Nowadays I feel so good about ageing and spreading my wings to do things I never had time to do when I was younger.

*Andie MacDowell*

I care less and less what people think. Not in a negative way, I don't want to upset people. But I'm not worried about my image any more.

*Kevin Whatley*

The best bit about growing old is that once you've ruined your reputation, people no longer have vaulted expectations in regard to your behaviour.

*Anon*

I don't much like being photographed without make-up, but I don't find fame at my level a burden. One of the good things about getting older is that you worry less about what people think of you.

*Victoria Wood*

# The Perks of Getting Older

Great thing about getting older is you can say what you want… You're not rude anymore… it's character.

*Jack Dee*

One of the great advantages of getting older is that you can walk into a world which is more truthful and less to do with other people's fantasies.

*Helen Mirren*

Forget all the advertising crap about the golden years; that's just bull – to try to get you to put your money into real estate.

*Eric Idle*

I'm grown up now and I manage to appear as if I'm not shy.

*Joan Armatrading*

Just keep pissing in your pajamas and complaining about everything. That's the great benefit of old age.

*Eric Idle*

Now I'm a strong lady. I think nothing of flying around the world on my own.

*Cilla Black*

I'm more tolerant now and worry about the little things less. I used to think I was a pessimist, but the opposite is true. You could dump 10 tonnes of shit on me and I wouldn't be fazed.

*Paul O'Grady*

# The Perks of Getting Older

I don't think I ever felt beautiful until I was pregnant
and when I gave birth to my children. (I had terrible
acne when I was a teenager, and I was very tall, so tall I
couldn't see myself in my mother's long mirror.)

*Vanessa Redgrave*

All their lives, they've been somebody's daughter, then
somebody's wife, then somebody's mother, and never
really had an independent life. They are thought of as
well-behaved, not having any kind of desires. At the end
of their life, they finally get to be who they want to be.
And they're filthy.

*Meera Syal*

A major advantage of age is learning to accept people
without passing judgment.

*Liz Carpenter*

As you grow older, you'll find that you enjoy talking to
strangers far more than to your friends.

*Joy Williams*

The older I get, the less important the comma becomes.
Let the reader catch his own breath.

*Elizabeth Clarkson Zwart*

I find women growing older attractive – I like their faces.

*Annette Bening*

As you get older, it's nice to be able to relax a bit about
your appearance. Writing does that for me. It comes

from inside me, from my brain and from my heart, and hopefully it has much more value than anything that's on the exterior.

*Emma Samms*

I no longer worry about growing old, because it has been a lot more enjoyable than I thought. It's true that those who live longest know the most, and I'm infinitely wiser than I used to be. There is also that Sophoclean thing about having untied those great, ugly chains of sexual desire.

*Ned Sherrin*

It's a relief not to have to be the slimmest and the firmest and have the highest booty. It's a prison, if you want to know the truth. I try to look good, but I want to look good for my age.

*Cheryl Ladd*

I love interviewing old people, because they literally don't give a damn what they say. Why should they?

*Michael Parkinson*

I am relieved to be older; to be able to gain a perspective that was elusive when I was younger… I think, "Well, for fuck's sake, I am fat"… I preempt it.

*Alison Moyet*

The good thing about getting older is that, as you become less attractive, so you have less desire to go out and conquer everyone you see.

*Julian Clary*

# Keeping Up Appearances

I am not nearly as afraid of myself and my imagination as I used to be.

*Billy Connolly*

When I was 20, 25, even 30, I wouldn't think twice about the consequences of what I said and now I think I'm much more measured.

*Sandra Bernhard*

# Keeping Up Appearances

I've always been in control of my life. I've always looked after myself. I'm so vain.

*Rod Stewart*

I remember one time when I played football with him, afterwards in the changing room, we all looked on in mocking disbelief, as he carefully gelled his hair and then applied moisturiser to his face. Now I look back and see how good he still looks, how he's hardly changed a day, I think Rod [Stewart] has had the last laugh on all us silly little boys.

*Chris Evans*

Just have as much luck as I've had.

*Paul Newman*

However much some journalists may criticize me, I know that I look, feel and behave several decades younger than my actual age, and much of that is because I believe you are what you think you are.

*Joan Collins,* The Art of Living Well

# Keeping Up Appearances

A love of life, spaghetti and the odd bath in virgin olive oil.

*Sophia Loren's beauty secrets*

Don't smoke, don't smoke!

*Susan Sarandon, on the secret of good skin*

I try to drink a glass of champagne every morning – it's penicillin for the soul.

*John Mortimer*

With a drink it is better. I am very fun after one glass of vodka. I am more beautiful, too.

*Carine Roitfeld, editor of* French Vogue

I looked in the mirror a million times, especially after drinking too much the night before, and thought I looked terrible, but now I stick to champagne; it doesn't seem to do so much damage.

*Honor Blackman*

There's a reason why 40, 50 and 60 don't look the way they used to and it's not because of feminism or better living through exercise. It's because of hair dye. In the 1950s only 7% of American women dyed their hair; today there are parts of Manhattan and Los Angeles where there are no grey-haired women at all.

*Nora Ephron,* I Feel Bad About My Neck

I do think I am enjoying being alive very, very much.

*Emma Thompson*

# Keeping Up Appearances

Even in my wildest days I never went to bed without taking my make-up off.

*Ann Burdus*

Get into a position of authority – that is better than make-up.

*Barbara Hoskins, press officer at 10 Downing Street under Harold Wilson and Edward Heath*

People tell me that I look younger than I am, but I don't accept that. I think this is what people can look like when they're 71, if they take a bit of trouble with their looks.

*Joan Bakewell*

Eat well and sleep well. That will feed your nervous system and your psyche. As you get older, you look how you feel.

*Francesca Annis*

Exercise can be a fountain of youth, in that it can help slow down aging changes and help you maintain a level of vitality and energy that you might not otherwise have. But you just have to do it smarter, because your body is more vulnerable.

*Robyn Stuhr, American Council on Fitness*

I don't want to have bloody sleeves up there. I've got batwing arms. My grandkids play with them. And I'm so short. I want lines that work well. God, I'd love someone to take me up.

*Anita Roddick on fashion at 64*

# Keeping Up Appearances

I'm fairly lucky in that I've always looked like shite.

*Bob Geldof*

Everything you see I owe to spaghetti.

*Sophia Loren*

I have tried not to give up the game as I've become older. I go to the gym and I've been doing Pilates twice a week for 12 years – long before it became fashionable.

*Joan Bakewell*

How do I stay so healthy and boyishly handsome? It's simple. I drink the blood of young runaways.

*William Shatner*

A turtle neck sweater takes five years off a man.

*Anon*

I have a gym at home and a swimming pool. I also have a personal trainer, Elizabeth, who comes over for two-hour sessions. My sons won't allow a male trainer. I don't know why!

*Cilla Black*

Women seem to feel young if they look young while men feel young if they have a young woman attracted to them.

*Anon*

My advice? You wanna look 20 years younger? Stand further away.

*Jeff Green*

# Keeping Up Appearances

Clean living.

*June Whitfield*

People ask me, "Why do you last so well?" and I say, "Because I've always got an interest in life. From the age of 16, I've always had something to do and somewhere to go." I've worked constantly and I would miss it terribly.

*Honor Blackman*

I am disciplined in what I eat, but I'm not a maniac. My father was a theoretical teacher of physical education so I was brought up with this attitude that your body has to do a lot of things and you have to look after it. Some of that was bound to stick, but I have to say that it's a matter of being lucky genetically. Being built this way is an inheritance.

*Mick Jagger*

I'm not a size eight, but I can fit into a ten. And it doesn't bug me if I put on a size 12. Wear what looks good. Size doesn't matter.

*Cilla Black*

I've spent most of my life not thinking about my looks and it has served me really well.

*Michelle Pfeiffer*

I feel my most beautiful now. To me, feeling comfortable in your skin equates with beauty. The best beauty regime includes lots of love and laughter.

*Jade Jagger*

# Keeping Up Appearances

My big beauty secret is that I love and need lipstick. It makes me feel feminine even in dangerous circumstances, even in the middle of a war.

*Bianca Jagger*

I, too, look in the mirror.

*Eileen Daffern, 93-year-old campaigner against nuclear weapons*

As for stripping off now, there is no way I would do it. I mean, come on, I'm nearly 57, thank you very much. Who wants to look at a 57-year-old wobbling round the place? No thank you.

*Alison Steadman*

As we grow old, the beauty steals inward.

*Bronson Alcott*

The worst thing is a sudden shaft of sunlight and a mirror. And you think, "My God, I've been walking around like the Forest of Dean." If I were to lose my tweezers, I would die.

*Arabella Weir, Grumpy Old Women*

It's not guys that you want to look good for – it's the competition. I go out for dinner with those girls and it makes me raise my game!

*Cilla Black*

I'm finding now in my 40s that the less makeup I wear, the better. I think softer is better as you get older. With everything. Except men.

*Kim Cattrall*

# Keeping Up Appearances

I don't do that much to preserve. I used to worship the sun when I was younger – I'm a southern Californian girl, it was all baby oil and beach life.

*Michelle Pfeiffer*

As far as getting older is concerned, I've always said if I had to sleep upside down like a bat so I don't look like a basset hound, that's what I'd do.

*Sharon Stone*

They made injections from the embryos of black sheep – you just have fresh cells and it's perfect.

*Debbie Harry on her latest method of turning back the clock*

My mother advised me to take hormones to stay youthful and I followed her advice. It was a big mistake. My breasts were so painful that I was frightened if someone stood too close to me in case they bumped into me. It affected my outlook on life. I really thought I was going mad at times. I'm not sure whether it happened to me just because of the hormones or because getting older was something I did not want to face.

*Shirley Ann Field*

Every year I go to the Optimum Health Institute in Texas and spend a week living on raw food, live enzymes and wheat grass juice… I still drink a lot of champagne, though.

*Liz Brewer*

# Dedicated Follower of Fashion

You can't live your life twisting yourself into a pretzel in this perpetual, "Ooh have I got the right dress, shoes, purse?" That message to me is very damaging to the psyche.

*Sandra Bernhard*

Several years ago I knew I had to choose between my face and my body – I always knew I'd choose the latter.

*Madonna*

If I had thin lips I could never express myself the way I'm able to express myself: with a kind of passion… A sexy, power-pout loud mouth!

*Sandra Bernhard*

# Dedicated Follower of Fashion

At some point in your 40s… someone comes in the middle of the night and nicks your dress sense.

*Jasper Carrott*

I used to do this thing in my shows. I used to say I knew when I was getting older when I'd walk past a rack of Dr Scholl sandals and think, "Ooh, they look comfy." Now I think, "Too modern, too modern."

*Victoria Wood*

I've embraced certain parts of getting older, like the sensible clothes culture. That's quite good.

*Roger Monkhouse*

# Dedicated Follower of Fashion

I can feel myself getting older. The problem is it creeps up on you like a Ninja. You think to yourself, "Ooh, I'm really young," then one day you catch yourself tucking your shirt into your underpants.

*Jeff Green*

I decided to start wearing one. I was surprised at everyone's reaction to it. Even now, people say: "Oh, you have an earring?" And I say: "So what?"

*Harrison Ford, about having his ear pierced in his sixties*

People make the mistake of thinking that because they look good for however old they are, they look empirically good. This results in way too many tank tops on women who are 50 and 60.

*Nora Ephron*

You do things you've never ever done before. Like, you'll be walking down the high street and just momentarily… you'll pause outside of Dunn &Co, and you're thinking, "Ooh. Nice cardi."

*Jasper Carrott*

Just wanting to be current, or in, or best-dressed or hot, seems to me to take too much energy.

*Kevin Costner*

I'm not minimalist by any means.

*Elton John on why he owns between 4000 and 5000 pairs of glasses*

# Dedicated Follower of Fashion

My grandmother, she had the life force. She had that extra power pack. She just kept going… She was an energetic woman. And then she got that gran coat. You know, at a certain age, you get a gran coat and a cake on top of your head.

*Eddie Izzard*

I try to keep things simple. I don't ever want to be mutton dressed as lamb.

*Jo Wood, wife of Ronnie Wood, guitarist with the Rolling Stones*

None of us, even on the sunniest days in 1934, went without his furled umbrella. The umbrella was our badge of office. We felt naked without it.

*Roald Dahl*

I suppose image at my age is a more subtle thing; being mutton dressed as lamb is a cliché I'd like to avoid.

*Toyah Wilcox*

At 55, I don't have to be on the pulse. I don't feel I have to be trendy or do anything.

*Chrissie Hynde*

I saw a picture of myself the other day when I was 14 or 15, and I was wearing a pair of bootleg cords and a polo-neck sweater, and when I looked down at what I had on, it was exactly the same sort of outfit. I feel I've gone all the way up a huge Everest of fashion gullibility and come right back to where I started out.

*Mariella Frostrup*

# Dedicated Follower of Fashion

The right clothes meant everything to me. I still appreciate good design, whether it's a bag or a pair of shoes.

*Paul Weller*

I am at the start of my mid-life crisis and doing all the stupid things that men of my age do to try and deny the fact that they are no longer young. I have bought myself Converse trainers and started wearing clothes meant for people in their 20s.

*Richard Herring*

I was a teddy-girl in Dublin and Peckham, a real rebel when I was young. I wore gladiator sandals, a white mini and a red duffle. I had to hide them – my parents would have killed me.

*Maura Haughey, 65, member of rock band, The Zimmers*

As you grow older you have to cover certain parts – your Madonna arms for example – and things such as miniskirts or baby-doll dresses actually make you look older than you are.

*Sharon Osbourne*

I tried thongs for a bit and I thought they were marvelous, because you've go no line, no visible panty line, which is kind of cheesy. And so I went into thongs in a big way. And I can't wear them now because I wore them so much I gave myself galloping anal itch.

*Dillie Keane, Grumpy Old Women*

When I go on tour, I take cases full of suits and scarves and shirts – all smart gear. A few weeks back, I was in the Oasis dressing room before a big show and they were all standing there waiting to go on wearing the same clothes they'd been in all day. I couldn't believe it. F****** scruffy northerners!

*Paul Weller*

## The Marks of Time

One thing sucks, your face kind of goes. Your body's not quite working the same. But you earned it. You earned that, things falling apart.

*Brad Pitt*

If we noticed we were getting older on a daily basis we would do nothing but squat in the dust and fret.

*Griff Rhys Jones*

I used to think I was quite intelligent, but the older you get the more you realise you're not.

*Terry Wogan*

It's ridiculous. I practically have no bum left.

*Julie Walters*

When I started using incontinence pads, I knew I was older.

*Josie Jackson*

# The Marks of Time

You have great potential when you're very young and very beautiful… I instinctively felt that it was a terrifying double-edged sword. Now I'm getting older and my so-called beauty will modify and be different. Then, when I look back at how I was when I was young, maybe I can enjoy it. It's sort of sad, isn't it?

*Charlotte Rampling*

I was a little more frenetic before. My stage routines have gotten a little slower, a little more paced.

*Ben Elton*

There's all these ludicrous things people tell you: that you can read more, when you can't see a thing, you can't find your glasses. And then everyone says, 'oh you can travel because you won't be working as hard.' Well you go for a nice long walk and then you have to go to the doctor because you've thrown your hip out. And yes, you are so much wiser, but you can't remember any of the things that you are supposed to be wise about. I probably could write my memoirs if only I could remember them.

*Nora Ephron*

A weird thing happens to male actors, especially movie stars, in my experience. They become grumpy old men. A young male actor feels great – all the girls want him, he's a star. As actors get older that sense of not being in control of their destiny grates on them and they get grumpy. They move into directing to try to feel a sense of control.

*Helen Mirren*

# The Marks of Time

Everybody has a year where they age a decade.

*George Clooney*

I know from experience of looking at pictures of myself that I don't like what I see – in photos it's not how I'd like to look or how I feel. Not least my big bust, which I hate and sometimes think of having an operation to deal with. It makes me look like a highly sexualised being, which I'm not. Though the legend lives on!

*Marianne Faithful on ageing*

I have aged, but I accept myself more as a woman, a pretty woman. Why not! When I was young, I did not develop femininity or elegance. I was a militant feminist. Today I have acquired several wrinkles, several kilos, but I feel better.

*Emma Thompson*

I think that your face reflects your temperament. A depressed person will look hangdog, but I have a rather sunny temperament, so I'd like to think that I look that way.

*Joan Bakewell*

Psychologically it's just not an issue. Physically I'm tired at the end of the day and quite glad to be reading in bed by midnight. There's stuff you notice like the skin on your face being less taut and you think "There it goes."

*Bob Geldof*

# The Marks of Time

As you get older, joints are no longer something to share, but something that sound like a breakfast cereal as they snap, crackle and pop each time you move off the sofa to reach for the remote control.

*Anon*

My photographs do me an injustice. They look just like me.

*Phyllis Diller*

You know you're getting older when fortune-tellers offer to read your face.

*Anon*

I'm getting older and my timing is better now. I don't speak quite so quickly. But I do get tired. I'm tired right now – but that's more a symptom of drinking too much than working too hard.

*Ben Elton*

I've apparently now reached the age where I've started to make involuntary noises around the house, which is quite good: I've waited years for a hobby.

*Roger Monkhouse*

I know my parents are retired now because they've discovered the switch on the TV set that only old people know about. You know that switch? It says, "Louder than Hell".

*Jack Dee*

# The Marks of Time

I've got really middle aged lately. I can't read the
paper… unless the woman in the house across the street
holds it up in the bedroom window

*Victoria Wood*

It only actually hit me recently that I was middle-aged
when I discovered I can't run. So I was going for this
bus, you see, walking casually along, you know. When I
saw this bus coming and I started trying to run, and I
realised after a few seconds that I was actually going
slower than when I was walking.

*Michael Redmond*

We lost my grandmother recently. She didn't die; we
lost her. She actually shrunk to the point where we
can't find her anymore.

*Dom Irrera*

Strange things start to happen and because it's not
consistent you just think, "Ooh, I'm losing my mind."

*Whoopi Goldberg*

I can't read the *A-Z*. Can't read the small streets. If you
don't live on a main road, I'm not coming to visit you.

*Victoria Wood*

I looked in the mirror one day and saw I was growing
me a hair in a place I didn't even know I had a follicle.

*Whoopi Goldberg*

# The Marks of Time

They say ageing is a funny thing. But there's nothing funny about it at all. You still feel 14, but when you turn on the bathroom light, this ugly old guy in the mirror leaps out at you.

*Eric Idle*

I sound like an old geezer! Well, I am an old geezer!

*Terry Wogan*

I have pushed the boat out as far as I should in terms of taking on too many things. I'm getting older and I just could not take it any more. I am now monitoring myself very closely and I'm just trying not to get into that sort of state again.

*Stephen Fry*

I looked down and noticed my "girls" had fallen. And not so much that they had fallen, but they had repelled down my chest. And the only reason I was sure about it was I was picking wood out of my nipples and saw all these grooves in the floor.

*Whoopi Goldberg*

I realize it's not too wise to climb that tree. And I can't play my beloved cricket anymore. I'm getting more and more used to my limitations, and enjoying them…. I quite enjoyed the hangover this morning. Do you know the feeling?

*Peter O'Toole*

# The Marks of Time

At my age the bones are water in the morning until food is given them.

*Pearl Buck*

One terrifying thing about getting older is you see your parents in yourself, for me it is mainly my mother. Now I love my mum and I respect her, but she is the last person I want to be and for years I've been trying not to become her, but in the jungle I felt she was metamorphosing in me at the rate of an infectious disease and I had to suppress every damned second of it.

*Toyah Wilcox*

I don't really mind getting older or looking older. I mind getting uglier and looking uglier.

*Chrissie Hynde*

Some people try to turn back their odometers. Not me, I want people to know why I look this way. I've travelled a long way and some of the roads weren't paved.

*Will Rogers*

Old age takes away from us what we have inherited and gives to us what we have earned.

*Gerald Brenan*

I'm getting older so I've started to smile more, because I want the crow's feet to go up.

*Simone Alexander*

# The Marks of Time

Childhood sometimes does pay a second visit to man;
youth never.

*Anna Jameson*

I was always taught to respect my elders and I've now
reached the age when I don't have anybody to respect.

*George Burns*

Of late I appear to have reached that stage when people
who look old are only my age.

*Richard Armour*

The "I just woke up" face of your 30s is the "all day
long" face of your 40s.

*Libby Reid*

I knew I was getting older when all the men I fancied
were over 50.

*Anon*

I get hot flushes, of course, and I become emotional,
but it's a kind of sweet thing when things really touch
you, you know? It's heartwarming, like the heart
opens up.

*Lulu*

I look in the mirror expecting to be 34 and see
someone who is 58. What's that all about?

*Deborah Moggach*

# The Marks of Time

I remember being shocked when I met an ex-student I used to teach and she told me she was 30! She must have left nine years ago! A little later I became used to bumping into graying, balding, fat old men at parties, who turned out to be ex-students. They were in their 40s and unrecognizable. Lately, one or two have come crawling out in their 50s!

*Raymond Briggs*

I don't run around anymore in a bikini at the beach. I don't need to, I don't want to. No one sees my hiney but my honey.

*Cheryl Ladd*

I'm getting older, so you're going to have to repeat the second part of your question.

*George W Bush*

Going half way up the stairs and thinking, "What the hell am I doing here?"

*Terry Wogan, discussing signs of getting older*

When you get the same sensation from a rocking chair that you once got from a roller coaster.

*Anon*

Do you ever go into a room and think. "What have I come in here for?" and you have to go back into the exact spot where you left.

*Paul O'Grady*

# The Marks of Time

As we get older we begin to see all sorts of signs of our encroaching senility, you know?

*Terry Wogan*

From years of doing Lilly Savage, I've got feet like Quavers, seriously… honestly, wedged in those shoes, I mean, it's not right. I look like Gladys Alewood has come round and unbound my feet on the Great Wall of China.

*Paul O'Grady*

My tummy looks like an elephant's bottom.

*Gaby Roslin*

You'll find a great difference [when you're 80]. The minute you turn 80, people will say, "Bless you."

*Roger Moore*

In the past, sometimes it would take me only four to five days to learn a role. Now it is taking me a good four months. My mind is so much busier than before, it takes longer.

*Placido Domingo*

You know you're getting old when you get that one candle on the cake. It's like, "See if you can blow this out."

*Jerry Seinfeld*

Nudity is a deep worry, if you have a body like a bin bag full of yoghurt, which I have.

*Stephen Fry*

# Growing Old is No Picnic

The Golden years are here at last. I cannot see, I cannot pee. I cannot chew, I cannot screw. My memory shrinks, my hearing stinks. No sense of smell, I look like hell. The Golden years have come at last. The Golden years can kiss my ass.

*Anon*

You will never find me relaxed about the passing years. I just want them to slow down.

*Bruce Willis*

But it's hard to be hip over 30 when everyone else is 19, when the last dance we learned was the Lindy, and the last we heard, girls who looked like Barbra Streisand were trying to do something about it.

*Judith Viorst*

Where is the path to Grown-Up-Land? How do I get there? Or will I just get old, not understanding that I am no longer young?

*Tish Grier*

Getting old really stinks.

*Martina Navratilova*

I hate it. I'd much prefer to be 40. People say you are wiser at 80 – well, I can tell you you're not.

*David Attenborough*

# Growing Old is No Picnic

If you live long enough, you're gonna get shorter.
What's the bright side of that? Hey, maybe some day I'll
be able to stand up in the back of the car again.

Dom Irrera

Men of my age live in a state of continual desperation.

Trevor McDonald

You can't run 100 yards in five minutes. You can't
climb trees. There are so many things you can't do.
I can't think of a single advantage to being this age.
Grandchildren, maybe, but you don't have to wait
until you are 80 to have them. So, no, 80's not all
it's cracked up to be. I wouldn't particularly
recommend it.

David Attenborough

Yes [I dread getting old]. That's why I had a lot of
children, so they'll be able to take care of me.

Ruby Wax

I seem to have spent my life looking at the clock,
watching time gallop away from me.

Bruce Willis at 51

Getting older is no picnic, and frankly I am against
it. Young people, be warned. There will come a time
when life narrows into a desperate rearguard struggle
against gums, hair, knees and any other body part
that decides it is time to hoist the white flag; a time

when if you nod off on the sofa, and wake up without too much drool on your shirt, that is something of a result.

*Martin Kelner,* The Guardian

Oh to be 70 again.

*Georges Clemenceau, upon seeing a pretty girl on his 80th birthday*

I tell you old and young are better than tired middle-aged. Nothing is so dead, dead-tired, dead every way, as middle-aged.

*Gertrude Stein*

In middle age, I practiced feeling old, but the real thing has been a rude surprise.

*Mason Cooley*

When you are younger you think middle age is old, but when you get there you think it is young.

*Anon*

I NEVER would have one of those put in. It's degrading. [People] sit there, like idiots, like they are sitting on the loo.

*A baby boomer, talking about a Stannah stairlift*

There is nothing that you can have when you are old that can replace being young and having nothing.

*Mary Wallace Smith*

# Growing Old is No Picnic

I reluctantly push the door slightly and peer in – posters advertising *Saga* magazine, walk-in baths and the merits of denture adhesive. Suddenly Dora Bryan waves and Thora Hird beckons from a Stannah stairlift. I pull the door closed and panic sets in.

*Marc Almond, facing up to his midlife crisis*

I don't want to be like a real old lady, I want to be active.

*Anon*

However light-hearted you try to be about it, the loss of youth, and everything that goes with it, is quite a trauma.

*Julian Clary*

If you're old and tired and you read the reviews and that's why you're here: beat it, because I don't need that energy, honey. I want the youthful, tapped-in, fresh sources, OK? Cos honey, I have kept my shit fresh for 23 years in this business. You don't see me dragging some old, tired, 40-plus ass up here, no honey. I'm giving up youthful, 19-year-old, optimistic, fresh, funky, on the cutting edge, on the tip, OK? So give it back. All night. Don't stop.

*Sandra Bernhard*

# When it All Starts Falling Apart

Beauty has no age boundary. What it means to be 50, 60, 70 is completely changing.

*Cheryl Tiegs*

My comfort is that old age, that ill layer-up of beauty, can do no more spoil upon my face.

*William Shakespeare*

Nothing is more ridiculous in old people that were once good-looking than to forget that they are not so still.

*Francois Duc de la Rochefoucauld*

Ageing can be very painful for women if they are judged by their appearance. It's about questioning what we regard as beautiful. Size ten and age 22 has become boring.

*Lindsay Nicholson, editor of* Good Housekeeping

Now that I'm old, my wish is womanish: that the boy putting groceries in my car see me.

*Randall Jarrell*

Getting old doesn't worry me. I'm not saying I don't look in the mirror. I do – and say, "Oh shit, look at that. The neck is going a bit."

*Barbara Windsor*

# When it All Starts Falling Apart

It's very hard having been so beautiful when young.

*Marianne Faithful*

A woman may develop wrinkles and cellulite, lose her waistline, her bustline, her ability to bear a child, even her sense of humor, but none of that implies a loss of her sexuality, her femininity.

*Barbara Gordon*

The body of a young woman is God's greatest achievement. Of course He could have made it to last longer, but you can't have everything.

*Neil Simon,* The Gingerbread Lady

It's every woman's tragedy that, after a certain age, she looks like a female impersonator.

*Angela Carter*

You start out happy that you have no hips or boobs. All of a sudden you get them and it feels sloppy. Then just when you start liking them, they start drooping.

*Cindy Crawford*

Getting older is not nice for anyone, not for men, not for women, and even more difficult for people who depend on their physical appearance. But it's not a drama. I know some people who are much more stressed than I am. And also, I live in Europe – I think it would be much more difficult if I lived in America.

*Catherine Deneuve*

# When it All Starts Falling Apart

I think it must be traumatic if you are a great beauty, because however hard you try to preserve your looks you get older – you must lose a sense of your identity.

*Barbara Hoskins, press officer at 10 Downing Street*
*under Harold Wilson and Edward Heath*

Well, I am not always going to be lovely, let's just face that fact.

*Madonna*

Nobody had said this tiny little thought: I feel bad about my neck. This is not profound. This is not "I think therefore I am." But nobody had written about something we all go through, which is that we feel bad about getting old.

*Nora Ephron*

I'm being stalked by my ass – it's gotten bigger since I hit 45 and there's nothing I can do about it – no amount of exercise will change it.

*Whoopi Goldberg*

I don't actually inhabit my body anymore. At some point somebody came along, body snatched, gave me this. It's the kind of body I used to look at on beaches and think, "Goodness me, how does that happen? How could you let yourself go like that?" That's how it happens – it just happens.

*Kathryn Flett,* Grumpy Old Women

# They're Not Wrinkles ...

Once you finally have the brains, the body is gone or going.

*Ruby Wax*

Men are okay from 30 to 45; if they're careful they can stay about the same. After that it's an increasing struggle because of jowl and necklines, even if the waist can be restrained. And the bruising of repeated sexual rejection starts to show in the eyes.

*Alan Clarke*

## They're Not Wrinkles, They're Laughter Lines

People normally get panicky about wrinkles… but it's OK: it's laughter lines. But then you see somebody's face like Keith Richards from the Rolling Stones and you think, "Nothing's that funny."

*Richard Morton*

Age should not have its face lifted, but it should rather teach the world to admire wrinkles as the etchings of experience and the firm line of character.

*Clarence Day*

I think being old is OK so long as you look right. I don't think there is any greater acceptance of wrinkles.

*Janice Turner, the former editor of* Real

# They're Not Wrinkles ...

Age wrinkles the body. Quitting wrinkles the soul.

*Douglas Macarthur*

You can put make-up on your face, and concealer under your eyes and dye on your hair, you can shoot collagen, and Botox, and Restylane into your wrinkles and creases, but short of surgery there's not a damn thing you can do about a neck.

*Nora Ephron,* I Feel Bad About My Neck

I've only got one wrinkle and I'm sitting on it.

*Jeanne Calment*

Sometimes I think your subconscious mind is going, "Oh, my God, I'm so old and wrinkly. I can't believe it."

*Emma Thompson*

I am lucky to have good Polish skin that doesn't wrinkle so I might be around for a few years yet.

*Ruby Wax*

It's not the wrinkles, but what they signify. It's about realising that you're nearer to death than birth.

*Jackie Sullivan*

I have days when I think, "Yes, you look really great Jo," and then days when I think, "God, I look awful, why isn't my nose a bit sharper and why isn't my skin better?" I'm getting older so I suppose I can't have that lovely young skin. But I think I'm doing fine for my age.

*Jo Wood*

# The Change of Life

Generosity, kindness, love – these show in our faces as
we grow older. And so, of course, do the opposites.

*Bianca Jagger*

Like many women, I'll buy a face cream that promises
to plump out my wrinkles, only to replace it a couple of
weeks later by another that offers the radiance of a
20-year-old. Hope springs eternal.

*Bel Mooney*

When grace is joined with wrinkles, it is adorable.
There is an unspeakable dawn in happy old age.

*Victor Hugo*

## The Change of Life

I don't agree with HRT at all, so I looked for an
alternative solution. I tried various supplements and
tonics, and even deep breathing to try to oxygenate
my body. In the end, the only thing that really
worked for me was a capsule containing soya extract,
called Isovon. One capsule, taken with an evening
meal, is the equivalent to about nine glasses of soya
milk. Within a few weeks, I felt like a completely
different person.

*Ingrid Tarrant*

My memory was the first thing to go when I went
through the menopause 20 years ago. I had always

been very good at learning my lines, but suddenly it was a real struggle. I tried HRT, which worked well for me. My memory came flooding back, so no more fluffed lines.

*June Brown*

At the time I went through the menopause – in my early 50s – I had no idea what was happening. I was driving when I felt a little woozy. When I stopped the car and looked in the mirror, I saw that my face was bright red. I went to see my doctor and got HRT patches. I was worried that one of the patches would fall off and attach itself to Robert in bed. It was a bit of a family joke.

*Babs Powell, wife of Robert Powell*

I have always suffered from crashingly bad PMS, so I am not looking forward to the mood swings of the menopause... I also swear by meditation. I meditate twice every day and this helps to keeps my moods under control.

*Sally Brampton,* Easy Living

My attitude is that the menopause is a natural part of life and you don't need to worry too much about it. Just accept it and remember that it does pass. For me, it now seems like a very long time ago.

*Anita Brookner*

The menopause made me so much warmer. I went through it when I was 52. I had some mood swings and

# The Change of Life

I was more forgetful than normal. But I think it helped that I led a healthy lifestyle and still do. I meditate every day; I do a lot of exercise and drink plenty of water. I also think that sunshine helps – I was living in California at the time.

*Lynne Franks*

At 46, menopause was the last thing on my mind. I felt young, healthy and vibrant. When I began experiencing unfamiliar symptoms, including mood swings and skin changes, it never occurred to me that I might be entering menopause.

*Cheryl Ladd*

I believe the menopause is a developmental phase. I'd had an early menopause so my need for adventure wasn't to do with that.

*Pamela Stephenson*

Keep your sense of humour. I remember watching a great musical called *Is It Me Or Is It Hot In Here?* Suddenly the menopause was really rather funny.

*Lynne Franks*

I love talking to women and getting it out of the closet. My grandmother whispered the word "menopause". We never talked about "down there".…. It's menopause – say it loud and say it proud.

*Cheryl Ladd*

Women know when they've got the menopause, but men don't quite know. They know it afterwards.

*Omar Sharif*

## Under the Knife

Infirmity worries me, but I'm not worried about having lines around my eyes. And I'd never have plastic surgery. They don't call it plastic for nothing, do they? Nothing moves. You can't show any emotion.

*Julie Walters*

I'm not against plastic surgery, I don't mind the idea of growing old disgracefully, but I'm terrified of the actual surgery and, for as long as I can, I'll stick with the creams and well-fitting underwear.

*Linda Barker*

I haven't yet had any plastic surgery. I'm not going to knock it … It's hard to be in this business… I'm leaving my options open

*Susan Sarandon*

I've had some facial surgery, which I think is essential.

*Debbie Harry*

Everything I've ever done to my body is self abuse.

*Sharon Osbourne*

# Under the Knife

The only parts left of my original body are my elbows.

*Phyllis Diller*

Actresses have to be able to frown.

*Catherine Deneuve, on why she refuses to consider plastic surgery*

My grandson has never seen me without a bandage.

*Joan Rivers*

I don't like Botox. It makes a very strange forehead.

*Carine Roitfeld, editor of* French Vogue

I'm getting older, which doesn't mean it's always a joy, but I would rather adjust to it than say, "I want to stay looking one age."

*Annette Bening*

It seems everyone in Hollywood is getting pinched, lifted and pulled. I'm looking weird because I'm not.

*Robert Redford*

I've had the same breasts for my entire adult life.

*Sharon Stone*

I've not had collagen injections; I just use lots of lipstick.

*Lulu*

I'm planning a face-lift. I have no qualms about telling people. I'm going to look younger so people will want to know why.

*Toyah Wilcox*

# Under the Knife

I went to see a plastic surgeon in Beverly Hills and he said: "You've got to be careful with your eyes." He advised me against having anything else done. He said I should try to look as natural as I can.

*Tom Jones*

I'd never cave into the pressure to have cosmetic surgery. I will not have Botox or fillers. The only time I'd have surgery is if I needed a tumour taken out. I just think that if you have good health, be grateful for that.

*Fiona Philips*

Better a new face coming out of an old car than an old face coming out of a new car.

*Joan Rivers*

Plastic surgery is a way for people to buy themselves a few years before they have to truly confront what ageing is, which of course is not that your looks are falling apart, but that you are falling apart and some day you will have fallen apart and ceased to exist.

*Nora Ephron*

I don't mind getting older. But if it all started sagging, I'd have the whole lot done again.

*Sharon Osbourne*

If God hadn't meant us to have cosmetic surgery he wouldn't have given us plastic surgeons.

*Dolly Parton*

# Under the Knife

There are huge changes in my body and my face, and I obsess over them. I just try not to have too many mirrors around. David [Arquette] has a huge problem with surgery, but I don't. It's hard getting older. It's hard not to be the young one anymore, to see your face change, your skin change, and not judge it.

*Courtney Cox, age 42*

I had my eyes done. Can you tell? I think it's important to look awake.

*George Clooney*

It's not as if I've had Botox or my hair dyed. I am still in original condition.

*Harrison Ford*

After losing half my body weight I had flesh hanging everywhere. I had the sort of breasts you normally only ever see in the pages of *National Geographic* magazine. So much needed doing that it couldn't have been done in one operation.

*Sharon Osbourne*

I'd like to be taller. I'm only 5-foot-7. There's lots of stuff on my top shelves I'd like to reach.

*Johnny Mathis*

I would consider surgery. Absolutely. Anything that helps. But it's definitely attitude and confidence that attract men. If you can pull without a facelift, why bother?

*Cilla Black*

Eddy: Look at Mummy, darling. Do I need surgery?
Saffy: Yes … get your mouth sewn up.

*Absolutely Fabulous*

You look like a million dollars. Is that how much it cost?

*Clive Anderson, to Cher*

The last thing I want to do is mess around with my face, not because I love it, but because it's me.

*Harriet Walter*

What's Patsy having? It must be difficult to find a priority on a face like that!

*Saffy*, Absolutely Fabulous

Michael Jackson looks great for 44, but between you and me, I think he's had some work done.

*Jimmy Fallon*

I like to use my face… that's why I am a bit apprehensive. That's what my husband likes about me – what he calls my mobile face – and I don't want it disappearing.

*Christine Hamilton, when trying Botox on a TV programme*

Women should age with dignity. The idea that you have this young face and a wrinkly body? It's gross! Why try and look younger than you are? Maybe you need a new husband rather than a facelift!

*Jerry Hall*

# Under the Knife

Cosmetic surgery… doesn't interest me. I'd rather have my expression lines and my ability to laugh.

*Twiggy*

One popular new plastic surgery technique is called lip grafting, or "fat recycling", wherein fat cells are removed from one part of your body that is too large, such as your buttocks, and injected into your lips; people will then be literally kissing ass.

*Dave Barry*

Beauty lasts five minutes. Maybe longer if you have a good plastic surgeon.

*Tia Carrere*

They showed this one beautiful picture of me recently and they had all the things that I had done. I thought it was a great compliment for everybody to think I've had plastic surgery.

*Cybill Shepherd*

The thing you notice here after America is how refreshingly ordinary people look because they haven't had their chin wrapped around the back of their ears.

*Sir Ian McKellen*

The trouble with plastic surgery is that after ten years gravity wins out and you have to have another one in a year or so.

*Linda Evans*

# Under the Knife

A woman went to a plastic surgeon and asked him to make her like Bo Derek. He gave her a lobotomy.

*Joan Rivers*

Plastic surgeons are always making mountains out of molehills.

*Dolly Parton*

It wasn't a fortune. It cost me the price of one-and-a-half Hermes handbags.

*Anne Robinson on her plastic surgery*

Cosmetic surgery is terrifying. It never looks good. Those women look weird. They look in the mirror and think they look great, but they don't see what we see. I think it's hideous. They scare small children.

*Jerry Hall*

I'd like to grow old with my face moving.

*Kate Winslet on why she would not consider cosmetic surgery*

It's hard to lose beauty. But I hope for grace and acceptance of ageing. I hate the plastic surgery culture and I believe we age according to the life we've lived.

*Bianca Jagger*

If I get a wattle under my chin in a few years, I'll have it surgically removed.

*Mia Farrow*

I've never considered a facelift because I earn my living looking old.

*Liz Smith*

# The Ageing Process

When men age they start to look like Clint Eastwood. When women age they also start to look like Clint Eastwood.

*Anon*

[My Mother] always said, "Don't worry about getting older, darling, nature has a wonderful way of maturing your mental faculties so that you don't mind the physical side of ageing."

*Helen Mirren*

Ageing is an interesting process. When I was 21 my life revolved around the right shade of lipstick. Taking an interest in other people is what matters.

*Carole Stone, former producer of* Question Time

You don't cross a frontier to old age – you just simply go on being you.

*Joan Bakewell*

Ageing is inevitable and, quite frankly, what choice do I have?

*Annette Bening*

# The Ageing Process

In old age we are like a batch of letters that someone
has sent. We are no longer in the past, we have arrived.

*Knut Hamsun*

Age seldom arrives smoothly or quickly. It's more often
a succession of jerks.

*Jean Rhys*

I'm not afraid of ageing. I stopped being afraid of life a
long time ago.

*Sharon Stone*

Old age equalizes – we are aware that what is happening
to us has happened to untold numbers from the
beginning of time. When we are young, we act as if we
were the first young people in the word.

*Eric Hoffer*

These are the soul's changes. I don't believe in ageing. I
believe in forever altering one's aspect to the sun. Hence
my optimism.

*Virginia Woolf*

My philosophy about ageing is that there is nothing you
can do about it. And it's better than the alternative,
which is death.

*Joan Collins*

The atrocious crime of being a young man... I shall
neither attempt to palliate nor deny.

*William Pitt the Elder*

# The Ageing Process

My youth is escaping without giving me anything it owes me.

*Ivy Compton-Burnett*

We are programmed to develop different tastes as we get older. It's as inevitable as backache and beginning to quite like the *Antiques Roadshow*.

*Sarah Dempster*

It was much harder for actors of my father's generation to age. They had these screen images they had to live up to. The whole star system restricted what they could do and how they could look. Ageing was a huge blow to my father's ego.

*Michael Douglas*

Old age is not a disease – it is strength and survivorship, triumph over all kinds of vicissitudes and disappointments, trials and illnesses.

*Maggie Kuhn*

The value of old age depends upon the person who reaches it. To some men of early performance it is useless. To others, who are late to develop, it just enables them to finish the job.

*Thomas Hardy*

With age comes wisdom... and discounts.

*Car Bumper Sticker*

# The Ageing Process

Growing old is no more than a bad habit that a busy person has not time for.

*Andre Maurois*

Age doesn't always bring wisdom. Sometimes age comes alone.

*Anon*

Many people think old age is a disease, something to be thwarted if possible. But someone has said that if any period is a disease, it is youth. Age is recovering from it.

*T C Myers*

I don't care what I look like in a film, but that doesn't mean I don't care how I look in real life.

*Michael Douglas*

Old age: a great sense of calm and freedom. When the passions have relaxed their hold, you may have escaped, not from one master, but from many.

*Plato*

Old age is not an illness, it is a timeless ascent. As power diminishes, we grow toward the light.

*May Sarton*

Sometimes getting older feels easy, sometimes it feels difficult. It depends how the wine is hitting you really.

*Rupert Everett*

## The Secrets of Thinking and Feeling Youthful

You can become so comfortable that your ends become blunted.

*Elton John*

I owe it all to drugs. It's nothing congenital.

*Ian McKellen, about his stamina*

I truly believe if you think yourself young, you'll convince others too. It's largely a matter of mind over cellulite.

*Penny Thornton*

Youth is not a time of life, it is a state of mind. You are as old as your doubt, your fear, your despair. The way to keep young is to keep your faith young. Keep your self-confidence young. Keep your hope young.

*Luella F Phean*

Playing golf with my husband [keeps me feeling young]. We've worked together and been parents together, but we became buddies on the golf course.

*Cheryl Ladd*

I have managed to have as much, or more, fun than many people ever get to have in their life, but I never forget the deeper levels of being a woman.

*Sarah Bernhard*

We can't hold on to our youth, but what you can hang on to is all the things we've been told a zillion times: you have to find the light in your life that you had when you were a little girl or little guy that made you happy.

*Goldie Hawn*

# I Can't Wait To Grow Old

I'll be honest with you: I'm actually looking forward to certain elements of my physical decay. I can't wait to have a good excuse to get in everyone's way.

*Jeff Green*

I can't wait til I'm freakin' 90. Just rolling in my wheelchair, in my pink terry cloth jump suit…

*Maria Bamford*

I think when I'm 60, I'll finally be cool: my old man's very cool.

*Bono*

No wise man ever wished to be younger.

*Jonathan Swift*

I have dreams of going back to America when I'm old. It's better to be old there. You get more for less money there.

*Ruby Wax*

# Young at Heart

I get to play someone 3,000 years old. I'm 23, so that's quite an acting challenge.

*Liv Tyler on playing Arwen in* Lord of the Rings

There is nothing more liberating than age.

*Liz Carpenter*

I'd like to be an old man with a good face, like Hitchcock or Picasso.

*Sean Connery*

After a gig I get to the hotel all psyched-up from being on stage and get stuck into *Homes and Interiors* magazine.

*Gary Barlow of* Take That

I aspire at some point in my life to wear a tiny pair of Speedos with a big beer belly and a comb over, maybe with a couple of medallions.

*Moby*

I'm actually looking forward to growing old, because for so many years I was considered a little kid.

*Donny Osmond*

# Young at Heart

I quite like being old. I've said this before and I'll repeat it: yes, I'm 74 years old, but in here, quite a lot of the time and in many instances, I'm 21. Nothing has changed, nothing has changed.

*Peter O'Toole*

My entire body starts to hurt: my knee, my back – but my head stays convinced I'm still only 23.

*George Clooney*

The interesting thing about getting old is that inside you still feel the young, spirited person you always were. You don't reckon with the fact that your body has become decrepit until it begins to let you down.

*Joan Bakewell*

Getting older is awful. I look 75, but don't feel it.

*Debbie Reynolds*

I thought my life after 70 was finished. But I could still keep doing things my way, with complete freedom.

*Minoru Saito, who at 71 became the oldest person to sail solo around the world*

I'm getting older but I feel kind of 18. I wouldn't want to be 15 again, but I don't mind being 18. Even so, I'm not daunted by the fact that I'll be 60 soon. It don't worry me.

*Roger Daltrey*

Growing older is not upsetting; being perceived as old is.

*Kenny Rogers*

# Young at Heart

Grown up, and that is a terribly hard thing to do. It is much easier to skip it and go from one childhood to another.

*F Scott Fitzgerald*

We are always the same age inside.

*Gertrude Stein*

You can only be young once. But you can always be immature.

*Dave Barry*

When I was 14, I was the oldest I ever was. I've been getting younger ever since.

*Shirley Temple*

A Jewish man with parents alive is a 15-year-old boy, and will remain a 15-year-old boy until they die!

*Philip Roth*

I feel much the same as I did when I was 11. I live in the same house where I lived when I was a boy.

*John Mortimer*

I still feel as bouncy as a 21-year-old.

*Lynne Franks*

# Turning 50

Oh this is horrible, the 50s. Oh, I am quite lucky. I have the same body when I was 20 years old. But when you are getting older, you have to find some new tricks.

*Carine Roitfeld, editor of* French Vogue

When I got to 50 I just thought, "Hold on: I'm thin. I've got my hair. I'm well off. I survived," you know.

*Bob Geldof*

I am in my 50s, but do not feel all that different from my 20s.

*Kevin Costner*

I've only been doing this 54 years. With a little experience, I might get better.

*Harry Caray*

Forty is the old age of youth, 50 is the youth of old age.

*Victor Hugo*

Yes, I'm 53 years old, but I don't think about it. I only think of what I must do tomorrow – that I must dance *Swan Lake*, that I must dance *Sleeping Beauty*.

*Dame Margot Fonteyn*

# Turning 50

I think middle age is the best time if we can escape the fatty degeneration of the conscience which often sets in at about 50.

*William Ralph Inge*

I don't mind at all. I have enjoyed every stage of my life. I had a series of events to celebrate my 50th – I was determined the celebrations would last the entire year.

*Baroness Valerie Amos*

It's just wrong.

*Paul Weller, on turning 50*

It couldn't get any worse. I looked like someone who shouldn't bother coming home from the cemetery. My hair was coming out in cobs and I'd lost two-and-a-half stone. I looked like a hunched-up old man.

*Paul O'Grady, after turning 50 and losing his best friend*

I'm feeling great – 50 is the new 40, without a doubt. But you can still be sexy at 60 – as women get older, they become more elegant and alluring.

*Ingrid Tarrant*

Fifty years old, 212 fights and I'm still pretty.

*Muhammed Ali*

Middle age: later than you think and sooner than you expected.

*Earl Wilson*

It's fantastic. I really love everything about it. I like myself more and I feel better about myself.

*Geena Davis on turning 50*

Fifty is the new 40. I always thought my best work would come in the years 40 to 60, if I was fortunate enough to hang around – and it is hard to stick around.

*Bruce Willis*

# Turning 60

Ageing doesn't bother me. I look at girls in their 20s and appreciate their beauty, but they are so self-absorbed at that age. When I look at 60-year-olds I think they look great.

*Andie MacDowell*

Some people reach the age of 60 before others.

*Lord Hood*

You must not pity me because my 60th year finds me still astonished. To be astonished is one of the surest ways of not growing old too quickly.

*Sidonie Gabrielle Colette*

The thing about being 60 is that you think about time a tremendous amount. You want to slow everything down and cherish every little moment.

*Diane Keaton*

## Another Year Older

I have no patience with the people who grow old at 60 just because they are entitled to a bus pass. Sixty should be the time to start something new, not put your feet up.

*Mary Wesley*

I reach the age of 60. Until about five years ago I detected no decline at all in physical vigour and felt as young as I did at 30. In the last five years, however, I am conscious that my physical powers are on the decline. I am getting slightly deaf and the passions of the flesh are spent.

*Harold Nicolson*

# Another Year Older

I don't call them birthdays anymore. They are anniversaries of your 39th birthday. And this would be the 41st anniversary of my 39th birthday.

*Ronald Reagan*

I never give my own age much thought. Whenever I see it printed in a newspaper, I subconsciously think, "That can't be right, it's impossible."

*Joan Collins,* The Art of Living Well

Today 50 is almost the new 35 and being in your 60s is comparable to how being in your 40s was in the 20th century.

*Joan Collins,* The Art of Living Well

# Another Year Older

I intend to live to a 100 and go down in history.

*Keith Richards*

Now I must turn my questing violet eyes to 1969. My 70th year! There is really no comment to make about that except perhaps, "Well, well", "Fancy", or "Oh fuck".

*Noel Coward*

I am not the first man who wanted to make changes in his life at 60 and I won't be the last. It is just that others can do it in anonymity.

*Harrison Ford*

I see it as a sort of liberation. Just the other day, I was talking to my neighbour upstairs about my birthday. 'Well, Kiki,' she said, 'now you can be a diva.' And it's true: age does confer a certain freedom on you. You don't have to play the game any more.

*Kiki Dee, contemplating her 60th birthday*

Anyway, if you can find me someone who IS getting younger I'll give you everything I own.

*Roger Daltrey*

The last birthday that's any good is 23.

*Andy Rooney*

When I hit 40 I thought it was going to be a dramatic turning point, but on the day I realised that the world hadn't exploded.

*Helena Bonham Carter*

# It's All Lies!

I remember thinking on my 30th birthday I was so old. It is hilarious now.

*Diane Keaton*

People say, "You've gotta do something Barb; you've gotta do something [to celebrate your 70th]." So I'm going to have a few of my favourite people… just a little something… I wanted to find a place that looked over London, because I love London.

*Barbara Windsor*

# It's All Lies!

Late 70s … very, very late 70s.

*Actress Liz Smith, revealing her age*

My mother was an amazing older woman, an extraordinary 70-year-old. She was one of those fantastically lively women who run up and down stairs all day. Actually, she was always telling people that she was older than she was, so she seemed even more amazing. That's a good trick.

*Felicity Kendall*

If a woman tells you she's 20 and looks 16, she's 12. If she tells you she's 26 and looks 26, she's damn near 40.

*Chris Rock*

So people think I'm lying about my age all the time? It's the records that are wrong. I've never told anyone how old I am. The minute they ask me, I say "That's none of your business." So that means I've never once lied about my age. Now that's true!

*Calista Flockhart*

Women who lie about their age look foolish

*Bel Moony*

## It's Only a Number

What most persons consider as virtue, after the age of 40 is simply a loss of energy.

*Voltaire*

Like beauty, age is in the eye of the beholder.

*Anon*

Thirty-five is a very attractive age; London society is full of women who have of their own free choice remained 35 for years.

*Oscar Wilde*

Age is a matter of feeling, not of years.

*George William Curtis*

Forty isn't old, if you're a tree.

*Anon*

# It's Only a Number

The woman who tells her age is either too young to have anything to lose or too old to have anything to gain.

*Chinese Proverb*

After the age of 80, everything reminds you of something else.

*Lowell Thomas*

I feel my age as an average between 39 and 99.

*Tom Stoppard*

In your 40s you start to rise up and by your 50s you had better have risen up!

*Lynsey de Paul*

Women have a passion for mathematics. They divide their age in half, double the price of their clothes and always add at least five years to the age of their best friend.

*Marcel Achard*

Just write that I'm old. I've told so many lies about my age I don't know how old I am myself.

*Ruby Wax*

Creativity and genius don't know nothing about age; either you got it or you don't, and being old is not going to help you get it.

*Miles Davis*

# It's Only a Number

The best age to be is the age you are now. Whichever age you are, that's the best age. I'm a very 'now' person.

*Joan Armatrading*

I'm 60 years of age. That's 16 Celsius.

*George Carlin,* Brain Droppings

At 20 years of age the will reigns; at 30 the wit; and at 40 the judgment.

*Ben Franklin*

I do my best never to think of my real age. In fact, I'm quite surprised to discover how old I actually am when required to give my date of birth to people who are protecting my security or providing me with essential documents.

*Penny Thornton*

I don't hide my age because I feel good in myself. My mother was very young looking, may she rest in peace. When she was 72 she looked about 50.

*Barbara Windsor*

Is he really 83? My goodness who would have thought it?

*Nelson Mandela, confusing Tony Blair and Tony Benn*

## Working Party

I once worked at a drive-in theatre outdoors. And the cars would come in and put the speaker in their windows and if they thought something was funny, they'd honk.

*Steve Martin*

Playing Ophelia at the Old Vic. That was in 1957. I got paid 3 pounds, 10 shillings a week. I was sharing with two other people and the rent was 9 pounds a week and we were to give 3 pounds each. So I was left with 10 shillings. What is that nowadays, 50 pence?

*Judi Dench, on her first paid job in theatre*

I began to realize how simple life could be if one had a regular routine to follow with fixed hours, a fixed salary and very little original thinking to do.

*Roald Dahl*

Nobody gets a nervous breakdown or a heart attack from selling kerosene to gentle country folk from the back of a tanker in Somerset.

*Roald Dahl*

Nothing is really work unless you would rather be doing something else.

*James M Barrie*

The price one pays for pursuing any profession or calling is an intimate knowledge of its ugly side.

*James Baldwin*

# Working Party

Hollywood just doesn't want to make the same pictures
I do, and I'm too old to change.

*Robert Altman*

When I was a kid, the adults in my house got up and
went to work every day, so I kinda do that. You know,
it's a work ethic; I think grown people go to work…
And I just got a great job.

*Samuel L Jackson*

They give me nice amounts of money for showing up,
so I go as often as I can.

*Samuel L Jackson*

I've always been a character actress. It was such a
pressure when I was younger because I knew I wasn't a
cute babe. But being young and Asian meant that
generally people would be looking for the girl running
away from an arranged marriage, with a long monsoon
of black hair, floating in the wind. Then I'd walk into
the audition and they'd go, 'Aaah, okay…'

*Meera Syal*

And after the [army cadet] course, I obviously
thought, if merit isn't rewarded then, fuck it, I'll go
and be a transvestite.

*Eddie Izzard*

I dress up as a middle-aged prostitute and do a game
show.

*Paul O'Grady*

# Working Party

I've got this job where I show off, play my favourite records and get free drinks, and I get to shag Zoe Ball. Maybe when I die there will be some horrible punishment, like spending the rest of eternity with Liz Hurley.

*Norman Cook, British DJ (aka Fat Boy Slim)*

Years ago my acting instructor told me that in order to play age well, you had to imagine that your testicles are made out of Christmas balls.

*Morgan Freeman*

There's a danger that when people, especially employers, know you are 50, they put you in a little box labelled 'dangerously near sell-by date'.

*Penny Thornton*

Reinvention… is something that I'm a great believer in. What matters is that you are open to every opportunity that presents itself, at whatever age you are.

*Twiggy*

Nearly all the things I do that are of any merit at all start off just being good fun, and I think I'm sort of building up to doing something else quite soon.

*Brian Eno*

I did a few things that I shouldn't have done, career moves that other people thought were great for me, but in the end I should have gone with my gut.

*Peter Frampton*

So, my style has hopefully changed over the years and it is more relaxed, and I do tend to smile and have more than one expression these days hopefully – which I didn't at the beginning.

*Jo Brand*

I don't worry about showbiz. It's not in great shape… but my concern is making a living. I'm just thankful that I established myself as an artist 30 years ago and continued to stay on that path.

*Sandra Bernhard*

I've never admired singing, because it's been so easy. That's maybe why I never felt I'd proved myself, because in my family, to be proud, you bled and you sweated – and singing was just something I could open my mouth and do.

*Alison Moyet*

Without [Mike Leigh] I could be working in a store on a zimmer frame… he picked me up off the floor and turned my life upside down.

*Liz Smith*

I've often thought that people reach the top of the tree because they haven't quite got the qualifications to detain them at the bottom. A very good lawyer tends to stay in the law. The one who's not quite as gifted becomes Richard Nixon.

*Peter Ustinov*

## Successful Living

I was Princess Anne's assistant for a while, but I chucked that in because it was obvious they were never going to make me Princess Anne no matter how well I did the job. It was a question of who you were, rather than how well you did, and I hate that.

*Hugh Laurie,* A Bit of Fry and Laurie

Try as I might, I could not look at an overhead projection of a growth profit matrix and stay conscious.

*Boris Johnson, explaining why he quit his job after a week*

## Successful Living

You should never have ambitions, because you either achieve them, in which case, so what; or you don't, in which case you have a life of disappointment.

*Jeremy Clarkson*

I'd love to be a pop idol. Of course, my groupies are now between 40 and 50.

*Kevin Bacon*

The most satisfaction has to come from the fact that one way or another I have proved the critics wrong. I am still here and they have mostly disappeared up the infamy of their arse-holes.

*Toyah Wilcox*

# Successful Living

You've achieved success in your field when you don't know whether what you're doing is work or play.

*Warren Beatty*

For you to be successful, sacrifices must be made. It's better that they are made by others, but failing that, you'll have to make them yourself.

*Rita Mae Brown*

At the age of six I wanted to be a cook. At seven I wanted to be Napoleon. And my ambition has been growing steadily ever since.

*Salvador Dali*

I have a perverse hope that by the time I'm in my 60s I will be critically accepted and like your Dame Judi Denches and Dame Maggie Smiths.

*Toyah Wilcox*

I think one of the reasons that I've lasted as long as I have – touch wood – is that I'm no bother.

*June Whitfield*

I've always swung more from the seat of my pants. I love jazz and that sense of improvisation. I like to think I've had one long jazz solo.

*Clint Eastwood*

I'm delighted to have endured, to have survived, and to still be here and be capable of doing more work.

*Elliot Gould*

# Successful Living

Success genuinely surprises me. Where fiction is concerned, I still have the feeling that I've been allowed to play with the grown-ups.

*Alan Titchmarsh*

[My proudest achievement is] surviving. In a business where most people wouldn't last 26 months I've survived 26 years.

*Eamonn Holmes*

I think it's my curiosity that's given me longevity.

*Meera Syal*

I enjoy the times I'm not working as much as I enjoy the work. And it's nice to be a little bit exclusive. I think the best measure of success is that you don't have to work all the time.

*Paul Merton*

I remember telling my first wife – my eldest son's mother – I said, "As fabulous as you are, I got ahead of you in motion pictures. I lapped you like if it was a race."

*Elliot Gould*

Much of success in life comes from being able to put yourself in the shoes of another: in the shoes of a prince or a pauper, a dictator or a dick-head, a burgomaster or a burger-flipper, regardless of degree, status or esteem, it's what imagination means.

*Stephen Fry*

I have always yearned to be a guest on *Desert Island Discs*, though sadly I have never been asked.

*Alexi Sayle*

People from Yorkshire are very proud of their underachievement. You see these old fellas in the pub going: 'I've had a great life, me. Gone nowhere. Done fuck all. Aye.'

*Paul Tonkinson*

At the drabber moments of my life (swilling some excrement from the steps, for instance, or rooting with a bent coat-hanger down a blocked sink) thoughts occur like "I bet Tom Stoppard doesn't have to do this" or "There is no doubt David Hare would have deputed this to an underling."

*Alan Bennett*

## Awards and Recognition

I love being called [Dame Shirley], there's a special ring to it and it's so much better than plain Miss Bassey.

*Dame Shirley Bassey*

Fantastic. It's the recognition of a life. I thought it was great. I loved every minute of it. I love being a knight. I never insist on anyone calling me "Sir." That's not the point of it.

*Michael Caine*

# Awards and Recognition

I thought it was ludicrous to take one of those gongs from the establishment… it's not what the Stones is about, is it? I don't want to step out on stage with someone wearing a fucking coronet and sporting the old ermine. I told Mick, it's a fucking paltry honour.

*Keith Richards, commenting on Mick Jagger's knighthood*

I can't bring myself to use the title or even believe it of myself.

*Helen Mirren*

I hope this honour opens the path to allow me to be more radical.

*Anita Roddick*

We are the one English group who stayed all through the 70s. The one group who never left as tax exiles. I haven't even got a CDM (that's Cadbury's Dairy Milk, kids), let alone an MBE.

*Roger Daltrey*

Obviously my parents were there, my sister, my brother, an uncle came over from the States, an aunt from Trinidad, a cousin from Guyana… They were very proud. Now when they tease me, I'm called "the baroness".

*Baroness Valerie Amos*

It's just a very English sort of trajectory, the kind you can see, for example, in probably a lot of politicians in government who started out as rebels.

*Mick Jagger, on his rise from notoriety to knighthood*

It would be thrilling, yeah [to be knighted]. But then I'd be like Harry Secombe. I would never, ever use it and just be Harry still. I'd still be Rolf.

*Rolf Harris*

When I got my knighthood, I was very pleased that the government decided to give me that honour two years after I'd come out.

*Ian McKellen*

I was astounded actually – I had to sit down when the call came in.

*Baroness Valerie Amos, about being asked to join the House of Lords by Tony Blair*

As an Asian bloke, it's another thing I can stick on eBay. I'll do it tomorrow morning. You can look it up. I'll sign it, of course.

*Sanjeev Bhaskar, referring to his OBE*

For me it was about a recognition that Britain was changing, had changed – that we had people from different communities making a contribution.

*Baroness Valerie Amos, about receiving her title*

It's great for my parents. They're of that generation that came over here with nothing. My ancestors would never have believed that their offspring would be at the Palace.

*Sanjeev Bhaskar*

# Awards and Recognition

I really did all that for my parents. For them, immigrants that arrived with very, very little – my father had come from a refugee camp after partition – the leap in one generation was incredible. Not that I wasn't flattered. I wouldn't have accepted it if it hadn't meant anything to me.

*Meera Syal, talking about accepting her MBE in 1997*

I've been made a freeman of Limerick… I myself, personally, as a freeman now, will be able to drive a herd of sheep over the Sarsfield Bridge in Limerick as the whim takes me!

*Terry Wogan*

If there's any sense of an invasion, it's my job to suppress it. So I think a lot of people now will be sleeping a lot more comfortably in their beds, now that I've got my finger on the pulse.

*Jools Holland, discussing his appointment as Deputy Leiutenant of Kent*

I've won all the prizes in Europe, every bloody one.

*Doris Lessing, after winning the Nobel Prize for literature at the age of 87*

I don't want to be honoured. That means you're no longer in the trenches. I'm not ready for the award. I hate that.

*Joan Rivers*

This is all well and good, but I'm still bald.

*Larry David, accepting an Emmy award*

# Hanging Up the Overalls

RETIREMENT

I mean I'd like to keep my finger in – that sounds rude – my hand in – oh no, worse – but hopefully I'll be gardening, travelling the world by then, writing my novels. I'd like to think there'll be too much of real life going on for me to want to do much acting.

*Julie Walters, on acting in old age*

The point is, if I don't go to work, I don't have to get ready to go anywhere, do I… I don't have to learn anything and use my brain.

*Thora Hird*

What would I do instead of singing? Sure I'd become a vegetable and if I sat in the sun I'd fry.

*Shirley Bassey*

The idea of retiring is like killing yourself. It's almost like Hari Kari.

*Keith Richards*

The best time to start thinking about your retirement is before the boss does.

*Anon*

# Hanging Up the Overalls

Sooner or later I'm going to die, but I'm not going to retire.

*Margaret Mead*

When I joined this band, we thought we would last two or three years with a bit of luck and come out with a few shillings in our pockets. Now, here I am 30 years later, and I haven't done any of the other important things in life.

*Bill Wyman*

I can't wait until I'm 30 and I give up modeling because I'll be wrinkly and my bottom will be sagging…

*Jodie Kidd*

I'm not frightened of ageing. I don't like it, but ageing is a fact. I'm lucky, though, because, in France, interesting roles are still available to me.

*Catherine Deneuve*

I wish to die at my desk. I have no dreams about retirement at all.

*Penny Vincenzi*

I have picked up plenty of bumps, bruises and cuts over the years. I have injured a shoulder and torn a hamstring – that sort of thing. But I have got so used to taking a battering, on screen as in life, that I feel anything is possible.

*Harrison Ford, discussing making action movies at the age of 64*

# Hanging Up the Overalls

You have to keep taking on challenges. If you lose that, it's the end of you as a human being.

> *May Ushiyama, 94-year-old head of the Hollywood*
> *Beauty Salon in Tokyo*

I wanted to establish a way to live when I retired, not just survive off a pension.

> *Mitsuo Utsumi, 58, who took up farming in his retirement*

The motivation is that we are all running out of life and time to do things.

> *Roger Daltry*

I used to look upon success in terms of how much I'd earned each year. Then about 30 years ago I decided to measure it by the kind of work I was doing.

> *Leslie Phillips*

I'm thankful that I'm still busy, still in demand, and still coping at the age of 82. I must be doing something right.

> *Leslie Phillips*

I'm always very enthusiastic about things that I do, so I've got a reason to get up in the morning.

> *Ben Elton*

You know, I'm 70 years old. I have to get up at 6 o'clock in the morning and go do a load of rubbish with a load of people I don't like. I do it to stimulate myself.

> *Michael Caine*

# Hanging Up the Overalls

It's a matter of timing. Just before the tide begins to recede. There's always a time to stop. It sounds like heresy but, I'm sorry, I don't think Alastair Cooke should be doing his *Letter From America*.

*Terry Wogan*

I've had thoughts on it, and I'm going to do another two years and then they're going to have to shoot me. I think the public will have had enough. I'll be 68 by then.

*Terry Wogan (January 2005)*

I like to think of myself at home in the armchair, writing, smoking and occasionally wandering down the shop.

*Stephen Fry*

We realised we missed each other and decided that whatever time we've got left we want to make the most of it.

*Roger Daltrey, discussing the re-forming of The Who*

When you're my age and you see a story, you better go for it pretty quickly. I'd just like to get a few more novels under my belt.

*John Le Carre*

I won't be able to do what I'm doing forever. There aren't that many scripts floating around for 50-year-old chicks.

*Cher*

# Hanging Up the Overalls

I'm an old-fashioned guy... I want to be an old man
with a beer belly sitting on a porch, looking at a lake
or something.

*Johnny Depp*

I went to see Pete [Townsend] last year and said if we
ever want to do anything together we better do it soon
because in three or four years we'll be past it.

*Roger Daltrey*

Is it not sufficient that old people ARE something? It is
necessary that they must be forever DOING
something? The loss of the capacity for loafing is bad
enough in men of middle age, but the same loss in old
age is a crime committed against human nature.

*Lin Yutang*

Men and women approaching retirement age should be
recycled for public service work and their companies
should foot the bill. We can no longer afford to scrap-
pile people.

*Maggie Kuhn*

You know what is a nice thought? Retirement. That's
what we've got to look forward to. A 100 movies in the
can and time to relax on the warm beach.

*Keanu Reeves*

Before deciding to retire, stay home for a week and
watch daytime TV shows.

*Bill Copeland*

# Hanging Up the Overalls

My body will tell me when to give up. One day I'll be on stage and nothing's gonna come out in the right key and then it's over, isn't it?

*Roger Daltrey*

I do intend to keep working, even though I get knocked a lot of the time for what I do my philosophy is no-one knocks an old lady, so the older I get the more of a "win, win" situation I'm in.

*Toyah Wilcox*

There are only so many acting opportunities in a lifetime and I'm trying to get in as many as I possibly can before I go.

*Samuel L Jackson*

Of course, I don't feel old. But the reason that I still work is that I have always done it and it seems so natural for me.

*Johnny Mathis*

Do you know in 20 years' time I will be 65. Good god I hope I'm on a beach in Spain.

*Toyah Wilcox*

I'm just happy to be working!

*June Whitfield*

Maybe I said "I'm real tired" and it sounded like "I'm retired." Or maybe that's how I felt at the time.

*Chrissie Hynde, denying reports that she had announced her retirement on stage in 2006*

# Hanging Up the Overalls

There's so much more I want to do. I refuse to get to 50 and wait at home for the phone to ring. In Spain, actresses work until they are old. That's my plan.

*Penelope Cruz*

Don't call me, I'll call you.

*Nelson Mandela on his retirement*

Preparation for old age should begin not later than one's teens. A life which is empty of purpose until 65 will not suddenly become filled on retirement.

*Dwight Moody*

I worked hard all my life for this. Those who say I don't deserve anything, that it all came easy, can kiss my arse.

*Diego Maradona, shortly before retirement*

I just want to hang out on the beach and, like, not do anything.

*Chrissie Hynde, about quitting the music industry, 2006*

I don't plan to retire before I die. I don't like the idea of retirement. I don't want to play golf. I just want to keep doing what I'm doing. I do regard the playing of golf as like entering the antechamber to death. When my mates tell me they've started playing golf, I mentally cross them off the Christmas card list.

*John Peel*

# Hanging Up the Overalls

I decided to retire from show business at the age of 17, because I didn't like it a bit.

*Shirley Bassey*

I've got far too much energy to retire. What would I do? I'd go mad! But I wouldn't want to go on tour any more – it is too tiring.

*Joan Collins*

For all those lovely people at home that I get letters from all the time, saying, "Where is he, what's he up to?" – well, I'm alright, you see! I can walk without a frame, still got my hair, face hasn't been lifted, so – well – here I am! It's lovely being with you, and before I go, for all those people at home I must just say at once: shut that door!

*Larry Grayson at his last public appearance on the 1994 Royal Variety Show*

I thrive on stress, seriously. If I've got nothing to do, I start pulling my hair out like a parrot.

*Paul O'Grady*

After my wife, Ivy, died, in 1999, I felt the need for intense study. As I'm 93, it was a slightly unusual occurrence... I may just put my feet up now.

*Reverend Edgar Dowse, who gained a PhD at the age of 93*

I thought a dignified thing to do would be to live in the country by the time I'm 50 and write books.

*Jullian Clary*

Picasso didn't stop painting when he was 41 years old, because he felt he wasn't relevant, but he kept going and the paintings he made before he died are now worth 40 million dollars.

*Peter Frampton*

I love being an older comic now. It's like being an old soccer or an old baseball player. You're in the Hall of Fame and it's nice, but you're no longer that person in the limelight on the spot doing that thing.

*Eric Idle*

A friend of mine was thinking of giving up… She's one of the hosts on one of these, like, *Entertainment Tonight* shows. And she [said], "Should I give it up?" And I said, "Give it up? You hold on! And when they chop your hands off, you hold on with your elbows."

*Joan Rivers*

You never give up because you just never know what will happen.

*Peter Frampton*

# Life is a Challenge

SPORTS AND ADVENTURES

Years ago we discovered the exact point, the dead centre of middle age. It occurs when you are too young to take up golf and too old to rush to the goal.

*Franklin Pierce Adams*

# Life is a Challenge

I never want to give it up. It's been such a joy for me all my life… I'm too old now, I really am, to be an inspirational teacher. Because one of the things you have to do is occasionally demonstrate.

*Peter O'Toole, talking about being a cricket coach*

I knew I was finished – I could hardly see the bloody ball – but I went bang! And the ball went boom, into the river, in my favourite little cricket field, and I said: Pedro, get out now. And I did.

*Peter O'Toole, describing his very last game of cricket*

It's sex that keeps me fit.

*Dame Shirley Bassey*

I fell in love with fly fishing back in 1989 during a trip to Montana. Since then it has been a favorite pastime of mine – a pastime in which I participate more than I should and not as much as I'd like.

*Jane Fonda*

The uglier a man's legs are, the better he plays golf. It's almost a law.

*HG Wells*

I was only talking about my past, not my future. I wanted to challenge my dreams again.

*Yuichiro Miura, explaining why he climbed Everest at the age of 70*

# Life is a Challenge

I took up skiing in my mid-50s. I was anxious to begin with and, as I was slogging up the slope, I almost gave up. But I'm glad I didn't. Finally, I stood on top of that mountain, the combination of sun and snow absolutely magical. And then I pushed off. Fantastic!

*Kiki Dee*

Golf takes me out of the crap of a sick world. Golfers are genuinely courteous in a discourteous world. Show me a guest on *The Jerry Springer Show* who's a golfer.

*James Wood*

Fly fishing is a sport that the participant can literally turn into an art form, and nothing quite takes your breath away like standing in the middle of a mist-covered, forest-lined river just as dawn breaks or dusk falls, and watching your line sail smoothly through the air to gently uncurl on the water.

*Jane Fonda*

There are a lot of people who are capable of doing what I did. It's such a waste to have the elderly do nothing.

*Kozo Haraguchi, 95, a runner who runs 100m in 21.69 seconds*

That's another warning sign of old age: golf. It's nature's way of telling you you should be dead.

*Eric Idle*

# Life is a Challenge

If God had intended a round of golf to take more than three hours, He would not have invented Sunday lunch.

*Jimmy Hill*

I love going out on golf courses, and seeing the different terrain and different things that are out there. I've played courses that had alligators and deer. It's just amazing how much beauty and wildness golf courses offer, and I've played on courses all around the world

*Samuel L Jackson*

Although golf was originally restricted to wealthy, overweight Protestants, today it's open to anybody who owns hideous clothing.

*Dave Barry*

I hardly watch TV. It's partly about timing – I get home too late most evenings. But I do watch sport a lot. Anything! My favourites are cricket, football, tennis and athletics, rugby, golf. I have a problem with darts though – I'm not keen on that.

*Baroness Valerie Amos*

Golf is like an 18-year-old girl with big boobs. You know its wrong, but you can't keep away from her.

*Val Doonican*

The sense of accomplishment on a golf course is so great because it is you alone. You are responsible for everything you do right and for everything you do wrong. I kind of like that.

*Samuel L Jackson*

I am now 57 years old, I love running and try to run three to five times a week when I am training for the London Marathon. I have completed nine London Marathons for Barnardos,.I promised to run ten for them.

*Floella Benjamin*

I am as passionate about golf as I am about acting. I very seldom get angry at golf. The year I started golf I had a caddie and one day I did get angry with myself and threw a club. My caddie told me, "You're not good enough to get mad." I have never thrown a club since. I enjoy my golf, it does not matter whether I play great or badly. I let it go.

*Samuel L Jackson*

It's pretty much a daily routine for me. I'm finally at the point where I can work it out financially, golf-wise.

*Johnny Mathis*

The ball doesn't know I'm 47 years old. It's going, "No, please don't hit me!" I love playing tennis. I want to stay out there for as long as I can, and if you can still compete and people enjoy watching you, why not?

*Martina Navratilova*

# Life is a Challenge

I'd like to put on buckskins and a ponytail and go underwater with a reed, hiding from the Indians. I'd love to be pushing off a birchbark canoe in a forest. To me, that's sexy!

*Kevin Costner*

I've got a pretty good job and I've never wished I was a footballer. The football fan and the football player are two completely different animals, and I love being a football fan.

*Danny Baker*

I used to play a lot of football. At that time I lived for football. I just ran my arse off, playing left half and then right half.

*Eddie Izzard*

Middle age occurs when you are too young to take up golf and too old to rush up to the net.

*Franklin Pierce Adams*

By 78 you've done everything you're going to do. If you haven't bungee-jumped by the time you're 78 you're not going to do it.

*Karl Pilkington – Podcast Series 1, Episode One*

Fishing is very similar to golf, because in both sports you hold a long skinny thing in your hand while nothing happens for days at a time.

*Dave Barry*

# Life is a Challenge

When I was young, I did not see a single soccer match. Where I came from, football wasn't played. The sport simply did not exist… now some of us, the old guys, are beginning to understand how important the World Cup is for the entire world.

*George W Bush*

Golf… is the infallible test. The man who can go into a patch of rough alone, with the knowledge that only God is watching him, and play his ball where it lies, is the man who will serve you faithfully and well.

*P G Wodehouse*

Supporting Crystal Palace is a bit of a trial… My dad goes to every home match, and me and my brother go along too. We sit in the stand where my uncle used to sit. My aunt and uncle used to live across from the ground. We've sat there since 1969.

*Eddie Izzard*

Statisticians estimate that crime among good golfers is lower than in any class of the community except possibly bishops.

*P G Wodehouse*

Did you know I'm a kind of unofficial mascot to Arsenal? I get given tickets to all the games. I love screaming my heart out. I love hearing the fans screaming, "Gesty! Go, Gesty!"

*David Gest*

# Life is a Challenge

Be funny on a golf course? Do I kid my best friend's mother about her heart condition?

*Phil Silvers*

I don't just want to be around – I want to be able to play a round of golf.

*Cheryl Ladd*

I don't understand American football at all. It looks like all-in wrestling with crash helmets.

*Sting*

I never willingly chased a ball.

*Robert Morley*

I support Norwich City football team and when they lose I really don't mind, because I expect them to; but when we win I'm so happy – much happier than any Arsenal supporter could be.

*Stephen Fry*

I know people don't equate football with transvestism, but the fact is, there's got to be a lot of football players and football fans and people in the army, navy, airforce or driving forklift trucks who are TVs, because it's male tomboy. It's kind of like, male lesbians because we all fancy women as well.

*Eddie Izzard*

# The Box in the Corner and the Box on the Shelf

Nobody [in Britain] seems to have any gut feeling for what makes exciting television anymore, it's all management by numbers.

*John Cleese*

The Royal Variety performance has taken on a geriatric air. People you assumed were dead totter on the stage to wild applause.

*Richard Ingrams*

When you get on the edge of bad taste you will delight a large number of people.

*John Cleese*

I don't watch television, I think it destroys the art of talking about oneself.

*Stephen Fry*

This is not the golden era of British television… It's terribly disappointing, because it used to be the least bad television in the world!

*John Cleese*

To get on TV these days you need to be a young, attractive, lively thing who looks good in front of the camera – never mind if you can't string a proper sentence together.

*Barry Norman*

# The Box in the Corner ...

There is so much we can learn from TV. It's a window on the world.

*Stephen Fry*

It's awful to watch when people are being humiliated. Call me old-fashioned, but we are getting back to the arena, aren't we?

*John Cleese on reality TV shows*

Violence and smut are, of course, everywhere on the airwaves. You cannot turn on your television without seeing them, although sometimes you have to hunt around.

*Dave Barry*

I'm always amazed that people will actually choose to sit in front of the television and just be savaged by stuff that belittles their intelligence.

*Alice Walker*

Thank God we're living in a country where the sky's the limit, the stores are open late and you can shop in bed thanks to television.

*Joan Rivers*

Television is like the invention of indoor plumbing. It didn't change people's habits. It just kept them inside the house.

*Alfred Hitchcock*

# The Box in the Corner ...

Television is like the American toaster: you push the button and the same thing pops up everytime.

*Alfred Hitchcock*

One of the few good things about modern times: if you die horribly on television, you will not have died in vain. You will have entertained us.

*Kurt Vonnegut*

Television news is like a lightning flash. It makes a loud noise, lights up everything around it, leaves everything else in darkness and then is suddenly gone.

*Hodding Carter*

Back in my day television was live and not recorded, so what you saw is what actually happened… barely anything these days is live apart from the news.

*Greg Garrison*

Radio news is bearable. This is due to the fact that while the news is being broadcast, the disk jockey is not allowed to talk.

*Fran Lebowitz*

With electricity we were wired into a new world, for electricity brought the radio, a 'crystal set' and, with enough ingenuity, one could tickle the crystal with a cat's whisker and pick up anything.

*Theodore H White*

# The Box in the Corner ...

People in America, when listening to radio, like to lean forward. People in Britain like to lean back.

*Alistair Cooke*

The trouble is the BBC now is run by women and it shows soap operas, cooking, quizzes, kitchen-sink plays. You wouldn't have had that in the golden days.

*Patrick Moore*

I hate reality shows like *Big Brother* and *I'm A Celebrity*. I'd rather watch a goldfish bowl.

*Janet Street Porter*

I used to watch Doctor Who and Star Trek, but they went PC – making women commanders, that kind of thing. I stopped watching.

*Patrick Moore*

Television enables you to be entertained in your home by people you wouldn't have in your home.

*David Frost*

Imagine what it would be like if TV actually were good. It would be the end of everything we know.

*Marvin Minsky*

The only thing that's better about television now is the pay.

*Michael Parkinson*

Poor old Moira Stuart… that lovely lady who's getting the hoof because she's too old. That's outrageous! How old have you got to be now to work on telly? An embryo?

*Paul O'Grady*

Men don't care what's on TV. They only care what else is on TV.

*Jerry Seinfeld*

Sky Television? I imagine it's a bit like watching the *Sun* on video.

*Prince Charles*

In Beverly Hills… they don't throw their garbage away. They make it into television shows.

*Woody Allen*

There's nothing on it worthwhile, and we're not going to watch it in this household, and I don't want it in your intellectual diet.

*Philo Farnsworth, to his son, on television*

# If Music be the Food of Life

Do I listen to pop music because I'm miserable or am I miserable because I listen to pop music?

*John Cusack*

# If Music be the Food of Life

That old assumption that you have to be in your 20s is being broken. The pop hits are proving that people in their 20s, 30s, 40s, 50s, and more are up for the job.

*Elton John*

Age is a myth when it comes to rock 'n' roll. Why does age have to be an issue with our music when it's not an issue with any other form of music?

*Roger Daltrey*

All that bullshit about people getting older and not being able to play pop music – they shouldn't play because they're 50 – that's an insult to anybody who's 50, 60, 70, 80, or 90.

*Elton John*

Rock and roll – it's like a heart machine, it's gotta go up and down – otherwise, you're dead, you know.

*Keith Richards*

I always felt rock and roll was very, very wholesome music.

*Aretha Franklin*

As long was we can remain true to ourselves I don't see why we can't do our best music now. Musically we're more accomplished than ever.

*Roger Daltrey*

# If Music be the Food of Life

I didn't get into rock 'n roll for the women... but I adapted.

*Ted Nugent*

Now I know what all the fuss was about and it really cheered me up. But I also realize that I never quite got it right again.

*Chrissie Hynde, reflecting on the success of The Pretenders*

We're an awards industry now. It has nothing to do with rock 'n' roll. Rock 'n' roll isn't something you buy in the shops. It's the way you live your life.

*Chrissie Hynde*

There's more evil in the charts than in an Al-Qaeda suggestion box.

*Bill Bailey*

When you make a lot of money for a record company, they don't want you to evolve. Growing older, you naturally do.

*Alison Moyet*

[Pop music today is] so sweet, I feel like my teeth are rotting when I listen to the radio.

*Bono*

Boy bands should be exploded from a great height. They're just pretty people singing music written by others.

*Eddie Izzard*

# If Music be the Food of Life

I'm bored with music between 1955 and 1980. I'm completely bored. I can't listen to a rock and roll record. I can't do it. I would rather listen to hogs screwing.

*Sting*

I can't believe this is happening. For me to have recorded a song in the same studio as the Beatles is just so exciting.

*Alf Caretta, 90, lead singer of rock band The Zimmers*

Music at the moment is so dominated by R&B that people don't understand melody. They see holding a note as a kind of blankness, devoid of passion – because they see passion as just acrobatic vocal scales. But all that stuff is like having sex and watching yourself in the mirror at the same time. You're not really involved in the moment, you're just checking to see what your silhouette looks like.

*Alison Moyet*

It's very difficult to get myself or Styx or Foreigner, the older bands, on the radio. There's not a spot for us anymore on regular mainstream radio.

*Peter Frampton*

It is interesting seeing young people these days and watching how unimportant music is in their lives compared with our generation.

*Alison Moyet*

Peter Townshend shows us it's all right to grow up.
There is dignity after rock'n'roll.

*Sting*

# You Can't Take it With You

I'm part of a socialist tradition that means it is obscene
to die wealthy, so my entire life at the moment is very
intelligently dedicated to giving it away.

*Anita Roddick*

You can be young without money, but you can't be old
without it.

*Tennessee Williams*

Baby boomers are getting older and they have the
disposable income. It's a huge market if you get it
right.

*Twiggy*

Money doesn't make you happy. I now have $50
million, but I was just as happy when I had $48 million.

*Arnold Schwarzenegger*

Many old people receive pensions for no other reason,
it seems to me, but as a compensation for having lived a
long time ago.

*Henry David Thoreau*

Middle age… when a man is at the peak of his yearning power.

Wall Stress Journal

# Hobbies and Pastimes

I've never been into video games. But this is addictive.

*Flora Dierbach, 72, talking about Nintendo's Wii*
*interactive game system*

I have to garden and I have to write. They are the two most fulfilling addictions I know.

*Alan Titchmarsh*

I would be surprised if I read more than five novels a year – I prefer non-fiction because fiction is a real leap in the dark when time is short.

*Jeremy Paxman*

I'm 82 years old, so I missed that part of our culture. Soap operas, yes. Video games, no.

*Ruth Ebert explaining her recent addiction to Nintendo Wii*

There can be fewer more enjoyable things than a long drive when there is something really, really, good on the radio – a play, perhaps, or a serious investigative documentary where you learn lots of stuff to impress people with.

*Alexi Sayle*

If people concentrated on the really important things in life, there'd be a shortage of fishing poles.

*Anon*

My knowledge of gardening has increased with age, although I'm not as active with the spade and fork as I used to be.

*Terence Conran*

Getting older doesn't mean always you have become a better gardener or have more time to spend in the garden.

*Gwyneth Dunwoody*

I'm really good with books. I'm like a pit bull with a rag.

*Paul O'Grady*

My enthusiasm for gardening has grown as I've got older – I think it's because I know time is running out.

*Duchess of Devonshire*

I always loved going to those antique fairs, those big sales in a field. But I can't do that any more… It was fun when you could go… and bargain away. Now if I try to bargain, they look at you like they think, "What a cheap guy!"

*David Gest*

As you get older, you have more time on your hands. Some people do crosswords and others jigsaws, but I garden.

*Michael Winner*

One of the nice things about being middle aged is that I am free to choose. I can either join the old biddies making macramé plant pot holders or I can indulge in an orgy of sex, drugs and rock and roll. It's entirely up to me.

*Jack Shamash,* Good Housekeeping

I'm tired. Being older makes you tired. I quite like just sitting on the sofa.

*Liz Smith*

# Three Square Meals a Day

The scotch egg is such a Scottish food. It's as though a great Scottish chef said "I need a tasty snack. Let's take an egg... and wrap it in meat! Makes it a bit harder."

*Bill Bailey*

Every single day of my life I'm walking around in horror at the general acceptance of slaughterhouse practices. I've been tearing my hair out for 40 years.

*Chrissie Hynde*

I'm very aware of my figure and food. It's a natural thing because I'm a war baby. We were brought up on a diet of vegetables and very little meat. But my weaknesses are potatoes and chips.

*Cilla Black*

# Three Square Meals a Day

I do like to entertain. Not a lot; I'm not much of a one for dinner parties. I find them a bit of a strain, to be honest. Over six people and I panic. I haven't got pans big enough – and how many potatoes?

*Alison Steadman*

I lived alone and for 17½ years – from the time of my divorce until well into the 90s – I survived on a daily diet of tinned lentil soup and processed peas (plus the occasional potato added as a treat).

*Tony Blackburn*

My breakfast is the biggest meal of the day. The first thing that hits my stomach is boiling water and honey. If I have a proper lunch then I'll eat very little in the evening. It's about educating yourself.

*Cilla Black*

If tofu adds years to your life, they probably wouldn't be the best years.

*Garrison Keillor, US humorist/radio broadcaster*

When it comes to cooking, five years ago I felt guilty "just adding water". Now I want to bang the tube against the countertop and have a five-course meal pop out. If it comes with plastic silverware and a plate that self-destructs, all the better.

*Erma Bombeck*

I'm a postmodern vegetarian. I eat meat ironically.

*Bill Bailey*

## Going Places

There is only one difference between a long life and a good dinner: that, in the dinner, the sweets come last.

*Robert Louis Stevenson*

I never do any television without chocolate. That's my motto and I live by it. Quite often I write the scripts and I make sure there are chocolate scenes. Actually I'm a bit of a chocolate tart and will eat anything. It's amazing I'm so slim.

*Dawn French*

I'm a vegetarian. I'm not strict. I eat fish. And duck, but they're nearly fish aren't they.

*Bill Bailey*

# Going Places

So I rang Mum and Dad. They'd never been on a plane, never been out of England. I said to Mum, "How about flying to New York first class, staying a week at the Waldorf Astoria and sailing home on the QE2?" Mum said, "We'd love to, Pauline, but we've just booked our caravan holiday."

*Kiki Dee*

Americans who travel abroad for the first time are often shocked to discover that, despite all the progress that has been made in the last 30 years, many foreign people still speak in foreign languages.

*Dave Barry*

Travelling is like university without walls.

*Anita Roddick*

I like Florida. Everything is in the 80s. The temperatures, the ages and the IQ's.

*George Carlin*

I moved to LA for eight years. And then I went home. I got homesick. It never rained or anything in LA. It was never cloudy. There was sunshine every day. There's no weather. I got homesick for the weather.

*Michael Caine*

It is no coincidence that in no known language does the phrase 'As pretty as an airport' appear.

*Douglas Adams*

Whenever I travel I like to keep the seat next to me empty. I found a great way to do it. When someone walks down the aisle and says to you, "Is someone sitting there?" just say, "No one – except the Lord."

*Carol Leifer*

I don't go camping. I'm too old to sleep on the floor now.

*Alison Steadman*

I love Orlando [Florida] and I'm not ashamed to say it. Walking round Rome and looking at buildings… it's a waste of time.

*Danny Baker*

# Going Places

If God wanted us to fly, He would have given us tickets.

*Mel Brooks*

I roughed it once at Glastonbury, but never again. I was thinking "wait a minute, I'm living in a tent and crapping into a hole in the ground... isn't this why my parents left India!"

*Sanjeev Bhaskar*

Anything white is sweet, anything brown is meat, anything grey, don't eat.

*Stephen Fry, advising on airline food*

If Christ came back tomorrow, he'd have to change planes in Frankfurt. Modern air travel means less time spent in transit. That time is now spent in transit lounges.

*P J O'Rourke*

There are only two reasons to sit in the back row of an airplane: either you have diarrhoea or you're anxious to meet people who do.

*Henry Kissinger*

Queues of people; you can't get through luggage anymore; you wait three hours; they insult you and then take everything away from you! ("My cosmetics! This is for my face; some simple creams. There's nothing going to detonate here except me!")

*George Hamilton*

There are two seasons in Scotland: June and Winter.

*Billy Connolly*

It's not the destination that matters. It's the change of scene.

*Brian Eno*

There are only two emotions in a plane: boredom and terror.

*Orson Welles*

The Devil himself had probably redesigned Hell in the light of information he had gained from observing airport layouts.

*Anthony Price*

The great thing about Glasgow is that if there's a nuclear attack it'll look exactly the same afterwards.

*Billy Connolly*

We had tacky caravan holidays at Bognor when I was a child and I didn't like roughing it. I hated how the bacon would fall on the grass when you cooked bacon sandwiches.

*Richard Briers*

## Proud to be Gay... and Grey!

I suppose I'm a kind of icon and gay men do seem to love me. I've two in Barbados and four in Spain who look after me.

*Cilla Black*

# Proud to be Gay ... and Grey!

It took me 49 years [to come out]. I'm no role model.
Kids are coming out now at 14, 15, 16.

*Ian McKellen*

I think for the first time in my life I just found a man
attractive... don't want to shag him though.

*Danny Baker, after interviewing Richard E Grant*

Just as I don't want to hang around discos picking up
men any more, nor would they want me to. It nicely
avoids an undignified situation.

*Julian Clary, on the compensations of ageing*

Though trust me, all that's bi about me these days are
my bi-focals.

*Paul O'Grady*

He is living with the queen of premenstruality.

*Ulrika Jonsson, on David Furnish and Elton John*

I'm glad I'm not bisexual. I couldn't stand being
rejected by men as well as women.

*Bernard Manning*

I am the most well-known homosexual in the world.

*Elton John*

You've all heard some rumors about me over the years. I
guess this is the moment to do it. My name is Richard
Gere and I am a lesbian.

*Richard Gere*

Gay culture is youth-obsessed. I don't want to be the old guy wanking in the corner at the bath-house while all the young people have sex. But I probably will be.

*Rupert Everett*

It isn't over. There's a fight still going on. In some countries people can be put to death for saying that they're gay.

*Ian McKellen, about gay rights and homophobia*

'The Ancient Mariner' would not have been so popular if it had been called 'The Old Sailor'.

*Alan Coren*

# The Time of Your Life

Mindful that it's running out, I am determined to have the time of my life.

*Sheila Hancock*

This stage of life is so empowering – you become a bit like you were as an obnoxious teenager when you say things like, "I'm sorry, I'm not going to do that."

*Lulu*

I am enjoying myself. I have fabulous friends, a great family and am cherrypicking my next TV project.

*Cilla Black*

Maturity is the time of life when, if you had the time, you'd have the time of your life.

*Anon*

I get a lot of offers to do reality TV, which isn't me. I don't let anything interfere with my social life!

*Cilla Black*

I wanted him to talk about the universe, but he just wanted to watch the girls.

*Peter Stringfellow, discussing Stephen Hawking's visit to his nightclub*

## Going Back to Your Roots

I miss them terribly. They were wonderful people. They had a joie de vivre.

*Elaine Paige, talking about her parents*

The one thing I learnt from my family tree about my forefathers on my mother's side is that they were travellers. Like all actors, I'm a total gypsy. And I live in the moment.

*Robert Lindsay*

My head is in India yet my body remains in Britain. I straddle the world like a colossus. Like a 5ft 7in colossus.

*Sanjeev Bhaskar*

# Going Back to Your Roots

My dad's good. I think we're quite similar. We're a bit emotionally compressed; we don't get too elated by things because we've had bad stuff happen and more shit could be just around the corner...

*Eddie Izzard*

When I was a boy of 14, my father was so ignorant I could hardly stand to have the old man around. But when I got to be 21, I was astonished at how much the old man had learned in seven years.

*Mark Twain in* Bringing Up Father

I come from a family of losers and I've rejected my family as something I don't want to be like.

*Sting*

As soon as my mom would leave to go play bingo, I would blast the stereo.

*Eminem*

My mother was of a vanished age and it was only too late I realised how wonderful she had been to me, to the last... She tended to reminisce about her childhood with a certain romantic nostalgia; perhaps age will have the same effect on me.

*Marianne Faithful*

I was never much good at domestic work. My mother had a theory that if you didn't know how to do it you wouldn't have to.

*Muriel Spark*

## Family Values

I'm probably one of the youngest grandpas on the planet, but I can hardly wait. You know, they say it's fantastic.

*Donny Osmond*

I did not and do not think that children were for me. I have not changed my mind with age.

*Helen Mirren*

I'm still mastering the art of grandfatherhood. It's like being a dad, only with a little more corruption and mischief.

*Keith Richards*

I remember lots of people I've known, like my grandfather, who was wild and eccentric. He often forgot to put his shoes on…

*Ian McKellen*

I don't feel regret about the end of their childhood, just anticipation about their adulthood.

*Goldie Hawn, discussing her children*

Awesome. Incredible. Fabulous. Every time he calls my name, I just melt. He calls me go-go. He calls me go-go, and Kurt, he calls him go-gi. And he knows the difference. He's a genius.

*Goldie Hawn, about her grandson*

Never wanted them. Children need all of you; I'm not the broody type.

*Sue Barker*

I've always totally resisted the idea of being a grandad, but now I'm beginning to warm to it.

*Paul O'Grady*

I was very young when I first became aware that my mother was considered a great beauty. It put a lot of pressure on me. It forced me to rely less on my looks and more on my personality.

*Rhonda Ross, daughter of Diana Ross*

As a mother you have to have a view for now and a view for the future, and you have to try and work both, and to do the best you can.

*Vanessa Redgrave*

My grandfather always said that living is like licking honey off a thorn.

*Louis Adamic*

I phoned my grandparents and my grandfather said, 'We saw your movie.' 'Which one?' I said. He shouted, 'Betty, what was the name of that movie I didn't like?'

*Brad Pitt*

There are few better people to steal recipe ideas from than your grandmother.

*Hugh Fearnley-Whittingstall*

# Family Values

When Sharyn [his daughter] first told me she was pregnant I had mixed feelings, as you would. The word grandad! It brings to mind stairlifts, walk-in baths and all that kind of thing.

*Paul O'Grady*

There are but two families in the world as my grandmother used to say, the Haves and the Have-nots.

*Miquel De Cervantes*

I'm going to be a glamorous grandad! I was a bit scared about the whole idea, because I thought it would make me feel a bit old, but I'm over the moon.

*Paul O'Grady*

Well my Nan, oh yeah she gets things mixed up. She gets the hair drier mixed up with the telephone… you might have seen her around… wet hair, chapped lips.

*Harry Hill*

The older you grow the more you begin to forgive your parents for whatever mistakes they made!

*Annette Bening*

I'm not afraid of growing older – my grandmother was the centre of it all. I would love to be that person. The grandmother of the family, the godfather of the clan.

*Jennifer Aniston*

I don't have kids though I have such respect for women who do, especially boys.

*Kim Cattrall*

When you have kids, it limits you. That was a choice I made.

*Alison Moyet*

I'm not much of a family man. I'm just not that into it. I love kids, I adore them, but I don't want to live my life for them.

*Sting*

Becoming a grandmother is great fun because you can use the kid to get back at your daughter.

*Roseanne Barr*

I played with my grandfather a lot when I was a kid. He was dead, but my parents had him cremated and put his ashes in my Etch-a Sketch.

*Alan Hawey*

## A Man's Best Friend

I've had a lot of animals, but never met one like this. I don't look on him like an animal, just a bloody good friend.

*Leslie Phillips, referring to his cat, Mr Big*

# A Man's Best Friend

I am not a cat man, but a dog man, and all felines can tell this at a glance – a sharp, vindictive glance.

*James Thurber*

I gave my cat a bath the other day… He sat there, he enjoyed it, it was fun for me. The fur would stick to my tongue, but other than that…

*Steve Martin*

Dogs feel very strongly that they should always go with you in the car, in case the need should arise for them to bark violently at nothing right in your ear.

*Dave Barry*

I hope if dogs ever take over the world, and they choose a king, they don't just go by size, because I bet there are some Chihuahuas with some good ideas.

*Jack Handy*

Heaven goes by favour; if it went by merit, you would stay out and your dog would go in.

*Mark Twain*

In order to really enjoy a dog, one doesn't merely try to train him to be semi-human. The point of it is to open oneself to the possibility of becoming partly a dog.

*Edward Hoagland*

A dog, I have always said, is prose; a cat is a poem.

*Jean Burden*

A puppy plays with every pup he meets, but an old dog has few associates.

*Josh Billings*

It doesn't matter what you teach a dog, if you don't get up at seven in the morning to let it out, it's gonna poo in your bathroom.

*Ozzy Osbourne*

A dog is not intelligent. Never trust an animal that's surprised by its own farts.

*Frank Skinner*

No amount of time can erase the memory of a good cat, and no amount of masking tape can ever totally remove his fur from your couch.

*Leo F Buscaqlia*

## The M Word

I hate the assumption that people make about couples and stop treating them like individuals. I like waking up in the morning knowing I'm choosing to be with that person.

*Susan Sarandon*

I mean, as you get older, you think, "Oh, that's interesting. I'd really like to see that person again." You know, someone who tore your heart out and chopped it up and ate it with bacon.

*Emma Thompson, referring to ex-husband, Kenneth Brannagh*

# The M Word

Marriage isn't a process of prolonging the life of love, but of mummifying the corpse.

*P G Wodehouse*

Nine o' clock and Mr Excitement is in bed and I am watching *Desperate Housewives*… I said to him, "George, if you really want to end tyranny in this world you're going to have to stay up later."

*Laura Bush, wife of George W.*

Tim and I just celebrated 19 years together, which in Hollywood years I think is… 45. I think the key is just focusing on the present and not keeping one eye on the door to see who might be better.

*Susan Sarandon*

I don't get jealous. He likes to go to these clubs where they all get naked. I just sort of hang out and talk to them, and polish my nails.

*Trudie Styler, discussing her husband, Sting*

I took a good look at myself and decided that I wanted something different from the way I was living. That's not such a bad thing, is it?

*Harrison Ford, discussing leaving his wife and becoming a party-animal at the age of 60*

I was lucky with Paula [Yates] and I'm lucky now with Jeanne [Marine]. I never think of myself as lucky, but when you consider it, that's it, you know. I am.

*Bob Geldof*

I wouldn't be caught dead marrying a woman old enough to be my wife.

*Tony Curtis*

Only the other day, I realised I'm probably never going to get married.

*Kiki Dee*

When one of us gets a stiff hip, we'll have a bit of a laugh about it.

*Newly wed Liz Hurley on the perils of old age*

The secret of a happy marriage remains a secret.

*Henny Youngman*

If love is the answer, could you rephrase the question?

*Lily Tomlin*

Love is an electric blanket with somebody else in control of the switch.

*Cathy Carlyle*

I am a marvelous housekeeper. Every time I leave a man I keep his house.

*Zsa Zsa Gabor*

Everyone knows that a man can always marry, even if he reaches 102, is penniless and has all his faculties gone. There is always some woman willing to take a chance on him.

*Amy Vanderbilt*

# The M Word

I never mind my wife having the last word. In fact, I'm delighted when she gets to it.

*Walter Matthau*

My husband said he needed more space. So I locked him outside.

*Roseanne Barr*

She's been married so many times she has rice marks on her face.

*Henny Youngman*

It hurt me a lot to be divorced – more than I could have ever said at the time.

*Kevin Costner*

If variety is the spice of life, marriage is the big can of leftover Spam.

*Johnny Carson*

Never got married, never did the ceremony, you know, but we do kind of promise each other to be the best we can be every day, which I think is about all you can do.

*Goldie Hawn*

You have to be great friends and make each other laugh. We laugh a lot and neither is jealous of the other.

*Ruby Wax*

# The M Word

I used to believe that marriage would diminish me, reduce my options. That you had to be someone less to live with someone else when, of course, you have to be someone more.

*Candice Bergen*

Marriage is not just spiritual communion; it is also remembering to take out the trash.

*Dr Joyce Brothers*

Most people like to read about intrigue and spies. I hope to provide a metaphor for the average reader's daily life. Most of us live in a slightly conspiratorial relationship with our employer and perhaps with our marriage.

*John Le Carre*

An affair now and then is good for a marriage. It adds spice, stops it from getting boring… I ought to know.

*Bette Davis*

I like being independent. I like being his girlfriend. I like that notion. I think it's sexy and I do think that it's a way of saying, you know what, I don't own you and there's no paper that says that.

*Goldie Hawn*

Brought up to respect the conventions, love had to end in marriage. I'm afraid it did.

*Bette Davis*

# The M Word

It was a tragedy, that whole break-up. But we both knew the time had come.

> *Robert Lindsay, reflecting on the break-up of his second relationship after 15 years*

I think not getting married is something that happened. I've not been asked at the right time.

> *Baroness Valerie Amos*

I go on location.

> *Samuel L Jackson, on how he has sustained a 37-year marriage*

I was 24 when we'd married, a baby with the brain of a peanut. I didn't know what I was doing.

> *Robert Lindsay, on his first divorce*

At last I've got someone to take the rubbish out. And now I don't have to worry if the car goes wrong or a light-bulb needs changing. That's all marriage is, isn't it?

> *Meera Syal*

I still fancy Meera in her granny suit. At least I know what the future holds. Everyone in a relationship should dress up to be very, very old. It would help them work out how they will feel about each other in the future.

> *Sanjeev Bhaskar*

I always feel sad when I hear two actors are getting married. You just smell trouble.

> *Robert Lindsay*

I'm OK on my own. I don't mind being on my own, so long as I know I'm seeing somebody at the end of the day. I think we need people, I think we get good stuff from people.

*Paul Merton*

Old married people look so much alike that they have the same number of hairs in their ears.

*Albert Camus*

I quite liked being her boyfriend. We have been on honeymoon for 17 years and I am looking forward to many more good times.

*Des O'Connor, on marrying for the fourth time aged 75*

My idea of Hell is being totally independent without a man. Being an old lady on her own with her children grown up is not my idea of heaven.

*Felicity Kendall*

My husband will never chase another woman. He's too fine, too decent, too old.

*Gracie Allen*

I think marriage is a bit like a tightrope walk; you don't look down, just grit your teeth and keep going.

*Penny Vincenzi, on being married for 50 years*

There's only one way to have a happy marriage and as soon as I learn what it is I'll get married again.

*Clint Eastwood*

# The M Word

I have often wanted to drown my troubles, but I can't get my wife to go swimming.

*Jimmy Carter*

When you have someone in your life that thinks you're beautiful just the way you are, that's pretty nice. If I were a single woman out in the dating world, I might feel quite different about being 54.

*Cheryl Ladd*

[Mary] is looking fabulous. I mean the older she gets, the more beautiful she gets. She really does, I mean that. She really does; she looks gorgeous.

*Michael Parkinson*

I can't fly a flag for monogamy or whatever the opposite is; it depends on the person and on the situation.

*Sting*

I don't want to live in the past. I could have given it all up for a happy marriage. But now I'd really rather go for a drink... go dancing in Camden, listen to the Kaiser Chiefs.

*David Gest*

Now we are a family and we will never separate from each other until death.

*Pan Xiting, 106, upon his marriage to 81-year-old Chen Adi*

After my divorce, I used to go to jumble sales and spend three old pennies on a whole pile of old china, then go home and throw it at the wall. When I look back now I think that was healthy.

*Liz Smith, 85, actress.*

My wife said: "Don't try to be charming or witty, or debonair. Just be yourself."

*George W Bush*

I suppose this is what it's all about when it comes to it, marriage — reaching 60 and spraying each other with Ralgex.

*Victor Meldrew,* One Foot in the Grave

# A Fine Romance

I'd go out with women my age, but there are no women my age.

*George Burns*

When you're 23, you just want to shag anything that's walking. Now I want to be with my kids, with my wonderful girlfriend.

*Rod Stewart*

I thought she was wonderful then and I think dammit she's wonderful now.

*Michael Parkinson, describing the first moment he met his wife of 40 years, Mary*

# A Fine Romance

I'd hate to be alone when I get older. If the singing
stopped tomorrow I'd hate to go on on my own. I'm
still a romantic – that's why I can still sing a love song
with conviction.

*Shirley Bassey*

Elizabeth has great worries about becoming a cripple,
because her feet sometimes have no feeling in them.
She asked if I would stop loving her if she had to spend
the rest of her life in a wheelchair. I told her that I
didn't care if her legs, bum and bosoms fell off and her
teeth turned yellow. And she went bald.

*Richard Burton*

Sexiness wears thin after a while and beauty fades, but
to be married to a man who makes you laugh every day,
ah, now that's a real treat.

*Joanne Woodward*

A divorced man in his 50s will come wanting to meet a
woman in her 30s – they have that fantasy. Present him
with a 50-something woman's profile, including age and
a photo, and he will say no.

*Mary Balfour, head of Drawing Down the Moon, Only Lunch*
*and loveandfriends.com dating agencies*

There are plenty of men out there, but women have to
be proactive. Forget all those old ideas of "If it's right
for me it'll happen." Make it happen.

*Mary Balfour, head of Drawing Down the Moon, Only Lunch*
*and loveandfriends.com dating agencies*

Michael Parkinson: What do you look for in a man?
Joan Rivers: A pulse.

Days are more precious waking up with someone you love. I wake up with Molly [her miniature poodle] in bed with me and that's delightful, but…

*Carly Simon*

I can't be doing with any torrid love scenes at my age. Some of that goes back to my daughter Kitty saying when she was quite little: "Dad, we're not going to see your bum again are we?"

*Kevin Whatley*

Love itself is what is left over when being in love has burned away.

*John Hurt,* Captain Corelli's Mandolin

Ronnie is very good at complimenting me. If we go out somewhere with loads of people he'll always say: "You're the most beautiful girl in the room."

*Jo Wood*

Marrying an old bachelor is like buying second-hand furniture.

*Helen Rowland*

They're of a certain age, these ladies [his admirers]. You know, past their procreational best.

*Ian McCaskill*

# Toy Boys and Arm Candy

Love is the direct opposite of hate. By definition it's something you can't feel for more than a few minutes at a time, so what's all this bullshit about loving somebody for the rest of your life?

*Judith Rossner*

When you realize you want to spend the rest of your life with somebody, you want the rest of your life to start as soon as possible.

*Billy Crystal*

There's nobody special. I'm a terrible flirt and I just have fun. I wouldn't say it was dating, I don't do dates very well, but I do go out with men for dinner.

*Cilla Black*

It's a very strange thing to start dating again in your 50s. I don't think it's at all fun waiting for the phone to ring again.

*Lulu*

I'm still chasing pretty girls. I don't remember what for, but I'm still chasing them.

*Joe E Lewis*


## Toy Boys and Arm Candy

I've… tried younger men but I wouldn't recommend it, because they haven't grown up and they very quickly become rather boring and uninteresting. They just look good.

*Shirley Bassey*

Um, I seem to like younger and younger girls as time goes by. It's not that I'm getting older; it's just that they seem to get younger.

*George Lucas*

Guy [Ritchie] makes me laugh. He's gorgeous; he's brilliant – and, yes, he's [ten years] younger. I feel like he's my equal and that's hard to find.

*Madonna*

Yes, my husband [Reza Jarrahy] is [15 years] younger. We have a baby daughter, my first child. That's the real miracle, isn't it?

*Geena Davis*

I have never found that age made a damn bit of difference. I was 42 when I was dating Rob Camiletti, who was 23 at the time. It's a shame that older women are continuously indoctrinated to believe that they are undesirable, unattractive and invisible.

*Cher*

I was 20 years older than my last husband (Larry Fortensky). Age is irrelevant if people have a commonality of interests. I find being with a younger person promotes vitality, longevity and sexual prowess.

*Liz Taylor*

# Toy Boys and Arm Candy

One has to be able to count if only so that at 50 one doesn't marry a girl of 20.

*Maxim Gorky*

When a man of 40 falls in love with a girl of 20, it isn't her youth he is seeking, but his own.

*Lenore Coffee*

I hate young men. Cher, my good friend, she goes out with foetuses.

*Joan Rivers*

Power and wit are an ageless bait. It certainly is the glue that sticks the younger woman to the shrivelled old codger.

*Ruby Wax*

My husband (Percy Gibson) is 32 years younger than I. So what? It saddens me to think that people consider that a problem. It's trivial.

*Joan Collins*

English men are drawn to young, nubile women. I can understand it. I'd much rather have a younger lover than a 70-year-old man. They are much more beautiful to look at.

*Elaine Paige*

You never see a man walking down the street with a woman who has a little pot belly and a bald spot.

*Elayne Boosler*

# Toy Boys and Arm Candy

Younger men have the energy, but normally they don't have the intellect. And I have a rule: not to date anyone I could have given birth to! I prefer men over 50, but I am very friendly with a 45-year-old Liverpudlian.

*Cilla Black (at 64)*

My constant obsession is about getting older. I know that ageing is most people's obsession, but to make it worse, I'm dating someone who's 24. As they say, youth is there to mock you.

*Graham Norton*

It's only later in life that you know how to drive the younger man. When you're young, he drives you, often into a wall of despair, and this can ruin our little lives.

*Ruby Wax*

Is this my date, or did I give birth to it in the night.

*Joan Rivers, on dating younger men*

Harrison Ford, with his ear stud and inappropriately younger partner, Calista Flockart, needs someone to slap him round the face with an order of sushi before he falls too deeply in the theatre of the male menopause.

*Tim Lott,* Evening Standard

I found a lot of guys my age and older were absolutely terrified of me. Younger men weren't. They're full of "Let's go!"

*Kim Cattrall*

# There's Life in the Old Dog Yet!

SEX

It is our generation… the one that grew up in the 50s, that is silent about sex. Like girls of our time, we never even mentioned sex except obliquely

*Jane Juska*, Unaccompanied Women

Women of 60 can be intensely sexual… many are still beautiful.

*Paul Theroux*

Women stay sexually attractive for much longer than men now, and they know it. Their desire for sex outlives men's, too.

*Mary Balfour, head of Drawing Down the Moon, Only Lunch, and loveandfriends.com dating agencies.*

You could have the best sex of your life in your 60s and 70s… if you had never had sex until you were 60 or 70.

*Nora Ephron*

Being a sex symbol has to do with an attitude, not looks. Most men think it's looks, most women know otherwise.

*Kathleen Turner*

# There's Life in the Old Dog Yet!

We're all single in our fantasies as well, as the media constantly remind us. In a land where no-one wants to admit they're old, no-one can admit they're sexually unavailable either.

*Jeremiah Creedon*

I was so tired of seeing these stupid, cheerful books about ageing. One of them even has this whole thing in it about how you are going to have the greatest sex of your life in your 60s and 70s. Which is just garbage.

*Nora Ephron*

Only sleep with men you're in love with… or your husband.

*Joan Rivers*

Sex is like bridge: if you don't have a good partner, you better have a good hand.

*Charles Pierce*

I've always been told that I'm sexy. Although I don't know exactly what people mean, I do think I've been a woman before my time. I still like flirting and hope I will do when I'm 90.

*Honor Blackman*

When you tot it up, having 250 to 300 lovers over the course of 20 years only works out at something like a different partner every couple of months.

*Tony Blackburn*

# There's Life in the Old Dog Yet!

He's like a rabbit, he's terrible. Every song gets him in the mood for love. He's just like that battery advert – instead of that little rabbit they should have Ozzy's willy banging a drum.

*Sharon Osbourne on husband Ozzy's sex drive*

At 60 the sexual preoccupation, when it hits you, seems sometimes sharper, as if it were an elderly malady, like gout.

*Edmund Wilson*

I can't bear all this getting into bed with everybody. Well, it frightens my dog! But I don't like things like that – perhaps it's because I'm getting older. The doctor said to me, "Laz, when you're 39 you'll find that you've changed!"

*Larry Grayson*

I feel like I'm too old to just have sex. I mean, I want to have sex, but with somebody who really loves me.

*Teri Hatcher*

Police in Sun City West, Arizona, have logged more than two dozen complaints in a year of couples having sexual intercourse in swimming pools, car parks and on public benches. The average age of the perpetrators being 73…

Evening Standard

I believe in being sexy at any age.

*Kim Basinger*

When I complained that the firework display was over after an underwhelming two minutes, my wife said, "Tell me about it."

*David Letterman*

One of my big fears in life is that I'm gonna die and my parents are going to clean out my apartment and find that porno wing I've been adding onto for years.

*Bill Hicks*

# Silver Foxes and Silver Vixens

LATE PARENTING

Sally: And it's not the same for men. Charlie Chaplin had kids when he was 73.
Harry: Yeah, but he was too old to pick them up.

When Harry Met Sally

I never thought she would get pregnant so easy, but she bloody well did.

*The world's oldest recorded father, purported to be Australian mine worker, Les Colley, who was 92 years 10 months when he fathered a son*

[Being an older dad] wasn't an issue with my own father, as visiting friends always assumed he was the gardener.

*Tom Leonard*

# Silver Foxes and Silver Vixens

Women love me. I want to have more children. I can survive another few decades and want to have children till I am 100 – then maybe I will stop.

*Nanu Ram Jogi on fathering a child for at least the 21st time at the age of 90*

I don't agree with the view that men may father a child into their '80s but it's wrong for women to want to extend their fertility after 45 – that's ageist and sexist.

*Dr Gillian Lockwood, medical director of Midland Fertility Services*

What is important in parenting is not how old you are, but whether you are meeting all the child's needs and we are very confident about doing that.

*Patti Farrant on becoming Britain's oldest mother at the age of 62*

I remember coming last in the fathers' race at Samuel's school! They gave me a special prize for being a good sport.

*Laurie Forbes, on being a father at the age of 80*

It may seem glamorous to be a father after 50, but it'll put years on you.

*Cressida Connolly*

I'm good at changing diapers. I'm good with kids. So, I'm excited about it.

*Michael Douglas, on impending fatherhood at the age of 58*

# Silver Foxes and Silver Vixens

The problem with real older dads is that either they've never known the ghastliness of those early days and nights or they're so old that they've completely forgotten them.

*Tom Leonard*

I'm definitely good for it. My father Kirk is 83 and roaring along and my mother is 70 something and looking spectacular. So I hope to be around for a while.

*Michael Douglas on his and Catherine Zeta Jones,
plan's for more children*

I can't think of any other reason for living on the planet.

*Hal Riney, on the prospect of fathering a child at 54*

And here I am, 56, and by all rights it shouldn't be happening. But there's nothing we can do about it now. And I'm terribly excited about this. I'm scared silly about this. I'm going to be a father.

*David Letterman*

What I look forward to is when the kid is 15 and we go out in the yard to play ball. I'll only be 90.

*Tony Randall*

When faced with first-time fatherhood at the age of 49, I wasn't sure whether to celebrate with champagne or hemlock.

*Len Filppu*

# Silver Foxes and Silver Vixens

At 25 or 26, you're busting your ass trying to make a living. Later in life, there's time to enjoy fatherhood and do the job right.

*Hal Riney*

He opened a window in my heart and the light of the world shined in.

*David Letterman, who became a father at age 56*

I abandoned all hope of maintaining dignified order and wholeheartedly subscribed to laughter as a magic elixir when my son perfectly arched his urine stream directly into my ear as I changed his diaper. I would not have found that earful so funny in my 20s.

*Len Filppu*

By the time the child has trouble in life, you know, I'll be dead. I'll be long gone. By the time the kid's out stealing cars, you know, Dad will be dead a few years.

*David Letterman*

Having kids again this late in life is extraordinary to me.

*Larry King*

Some peoples' sperm should have expiration dates.

*Edward Lionheart*

The flag goes up the pole and everybody says, "What a terrific guy."

*Dave Hill writing about late fatherhood*

# Silver Foxes and Silver Vixens

I think the older you get, the more you can appreciate that you can bring another life into this world.

*Rod Stewart*

Today's 60 is yesterday's 50. As my kids grow, they will help me stay active, healthy and vibrant. I'll rock in retirement, but not in a chair.

*Len Filppu*

At my age a child is marvellous. My wife wanted it and I owed it to her. I said to her, "Here, this is what you wanted for when I am gone."

*Julio Iglesias, Snr on announcing he was to become a father for the fourth time at 90*

No doubt people will be saying how disgusting it is that a man in his 60s should be fathering a child.

*John Simpson, the BBC's world affairs editor*

As any little person tends to do, she wakes up in the middle of the night for various reasons and you want to ask them to go back from whence they came.

*David Jason, first-time father at 61, talking about his daughter Sophie Mae*

They can be old drunks with man boobs and back hair, but if they've got a babe on their arm – or in a sling – then they are a silver fox.

*Rachel Johnson*

I have a couple of grandchildren with my older boys and perhaps there are already enough youngsters in my life. But you never know.

*Harrison Ford*

Some women are great mothers at 20 and others are great at 50. If I had done it sooner I wouldn't be doing what I'm doing now.

*Ruby Wax*

A 90-year-old's sperm can, and demonstrably does, thrash like an Olympic tadpole.

*Rachel Johnson*

My grandfather's 86 and he's having a baby. Man, I hope when I'm 86 I can have babies.

*Enrique Iglesias*

It was the happiest [moment] in my life. She grabbed my finger with her tiny hand and held it – it was a gift from God… God willing, then yes, I would like another child.

*Adriana Iliescu, who became a mother for the first time at the age of 66*

# Comb Over and Out

HAIR

I am a Gray who is very afraid of dyeing.

*Spalding Gray, on why he won't use a hair dye product*

# Comb Over and Out

I was a natural blonde and when I got older my hair started to go dark, which gave me the willies, so I dye it blonde now.

*Honor Blackman*

Oh, that blonde. What a bore it was. And, oh God, the upkeep: I had to have it peroxided every week and it had to be blow-dried all the time.

*Catherine Deneuve*

Blair plays guitar and was in a rock band. For a brief period in 1976 he and I shared the worst haircut in Britain.

*Bob Geldof*

When a woman ceases to alter the fashion of her hair, you guess that she has passed the crisis of her experience.

*Mary Austin*

Ronald Reagan doesn't dye his hair, he's just prematurely orange.

*Gerald Ford*

Hair is the first thing. And teeth the second. Hair and teeth. A man got those two things he's got it all.

*James Brown*

Grey hairs seem to my fancy like the soft light of the moon, silvering over the evening of life.

*Jean Paul Richter*

# Comb Over and Out

Don't watch TV news. Look at those anchors in their wigs and ridiculous hairdos. Can you trust people who are lying about their appearance?

*Eric Idle*

Well, the thing is, it's always seemed to me that, if you're going to wear something on your head, why would you tell anybody?.. If…

*Terry Wogan – on whether or not his hair is real*

It's not a beard, it's an animal I've trained to sit very still.

*Bill Bailey*

The big difference between us and our mothers is only chemical. When my mother was my age, you could have two colours of hair. Blue or pink. Pink was called strawberry blonde.

*Nora Ephron*

I've been lucky with my hair. I couldn't deal with it if I'd run out of barnet. Imagine me with a Bobby Charlton comb over.

*Rod Stewart*

Unfortunately, with men, at a certain age, and it varies with different men, hair starts leaving. I didn't want to be one of those shiny on top, ponytail down the back.

*Peter Frampton*

## Toilet Humour

All my good reading, you might say, was done in the
toilet. There are passages in *Ulysses* which can be read
only in the toilet – if one wants to extract the full
flavour of their content.

*Henry Miller*

My aunt in Knoxville would bring newspapers up,
which we used for toilet paper. Before we used it, we'd
look at the pictures.

*Dolly Parton*

It's not hard to tell we was poor – when you saw the
toilet paper dryin' on the clothesline.

*George Lindsay*

Last time I was in Spain I got through six Jeffrey Archer
novels. I must remember to take enough toilet paper
next time.

*Bob Monkhouse*

Well, I don't use the toilet much to pee in. I almost
always pee in the yard or the garden, because I like to
pee on my estate.

*Iggy Pop*

You can flush my ashes down the toilet, for all I care.

*Carolyn Heilbrun*

# Toilet Humour

I'm shy. I can go on a trip for days and not go because I won't sit on a toilet seat on a plane. I'm certainly not going to go on somebody's lawn. Could you imagine, in a cocktail dress?

*Farrah Fawcett*

Turning 60 is not without its compensations. While it's true, for example, that my member isn't getting a proper supply of blood anymore – and that I can no longer write my name in the sand and must settle for my initials – I can still have lots of fun with it.

*Robert Levin*

Well, my wife and I were married in a toilet – it was a marriage of convenience!

*Tommy Cooper*

You know an odd feeling? Sitting on the toilet eating a chocolate candy bar.

*George Carlin*

When I was younger… I could piss from my bed to the bathroom… I didn't need to get up! I just lay there. Now I go to the bathroom, I have to hold the walls.

*Richard Pryor*

Right, where's me newspaper? I'm off to the khazi to try for a little baby of me own.

*Ricky Tomlinson*

In the olden days, when we had to use newspaper for toilet paper, Mr Merton would become so engrossed in a news story he would temporarily forget his mission. With the advent of soft toilet paper Mr Merton is much quicker about his ablutions, but now less informed current-affairs wise. Progress really is swings and roundabouts.

*Mrs Merton*

## The Battle of the Bulge

Curry, gym, curry, gym. Life's a constant battle between the two. I started going three times a week when I realised it was getting harder to stay in shape. I'd go on holiday for a week and put on nine stone. I'd eat a tea cake and put on eight stone.

*Lenny Henry*

It is an advantage not being pretty. I have no fear of losing anything except my figure, but that is difficult as I am very sociable and go out for lunch or dinner most days.

*Barbara Hoskins, press officer at 10 Downing Street under*
*Harold Wilson and Edward Heath.*

I've given up my stringent exercise routines of the past. However, I have continued with yoga. Yoga is a wonderful full-body workout which builds strength, flexibility and balance.

*Jane Fonda*

# The Battle of the Bulge

I'm not one of those obsessive "I must go to the gym" people. Jogging along a country lane is what I like.

*Sue Barker*

I always stayed fit because I'm a performer and all of those things help me to perform.

*Sting*

Health food may be good for the conscience, but Oreos taste a hell of a lot better.

*Robert Redford*

I had so much toast the other day I had to lie down.

*Jonathan Ross*

Stretching, stretching and more stretching, that's what we all have to do. As you get older your body wants to curl up, like a piece of bacon under a hot grill.

*Chris Evans*

I'm not into working out. My philosophy: no pain, no pain.

*George H Mead*

I really enjoy running and recommend it to all women over 50. Not only is it a great way to keep fit and have firm thighs, but it's a wonderful way to get some "me time", because you are free from all forms of communication.

*Floella Benjamin*

# The Battle of the Bulge

I have been through various fitness regimes. I used to run about five miles a day and I did aerobics for a while.

*Sting*

Fitness for young people is an option, fitness for old people is an imperative.

*Dr Walter Bortz*

Exercise? I get in on the golf course. When I see my friends collapse, I run for the paramedics.

*Red Skelton*

It takes longer to get into shape. Every exercise I did ten years ago takes a little more effort. But it is the only way.

*Bruce Willis*

I don't jog. If I die I want to be sick.

*Abe Lemons*

Apart from exercise and slaving over a hot pair of weights, I don't know any other way to avoid having bat-wings under your arms.

*Ann Robinson*

I employed a personal trainer six weeks ago who really puts me through my paces. I don't combine proteins and carbohydrates. I used to be fat and I'm not now. I never weigh myself.

*Ruby Wax*

# The Battle of the Bulge

The voice is different and hopefully it hasn't deteriorated too much. I don't feel old, but I find myself making sure that I can sing whatever I choose to sing.

*Johnny Mathis*

Only once, quite recently, have I thought, "I'm putting on weight, I must do something about it." It's because I'm sensible. I don't eat lots of biscuits and pastries.

*Honor Blackman*

My feeling beautiful has always been linked to being five pounds less.

*Natasha Richardson*

Eddy: Inside of me, sweetie, inside of me, there is a thin person just screaming to get out.
Mother: Just the one, dear?

Absolutely Fabulous

Eddy: The more I love myself, the more I will be loved. The more I love myself, the more I will be loved. I will be thin and fabulous, and live life every second to the fullest. This is not my fat. It has followed me from another existence. It is not the fat of now.

Absolutely Fabulous

I had a holiday mentality. I ate with wild abandon, six, seven, eight thousand calories a day.

*Kirstie Alley*

# The Battle of the Bulge

I'm developing a very good face and physique for radio.

*Eamonn Holmes*

When I was 14 I said, "I'm going to cycle from Sussex to Wales. I want to lose weight." But my dad gave me some money and a Little Chef map, which was the worst map to give me. I cycled from Little Chef to Little Chef, eating the maple syrup and ice-cream and orange fruities at petrol stations.

*Eddie Izzard*

The advantage of exercising every day is that you die healthier.

*Anon*

And last but not least: I don't exercise because it makes the ice jump right out of my glass.

*Anon*

A few people – and I see no reason why we should not beat them to death with sticks – manage to reach middle age with lean, slender bodies.

*Dave Barry*

A long time ago, when I was 20, you had to go on a grapefruit diet and then get wrapped in seaweed. What was I doing? Now I'd say: "What the hell is this seaweed bollocks?"

*Felicity Kendall*

# What's Your Poison?

It appears that the current stairway to heaven is lined with celery sticks. Everyone wants to be Born Again – three sizes smaller.

*Ellen Goodman*

Being thin makes you look scrawny when you're older.

*Jerry Hall*

I do diet, but in a smart way. I don't deny myself much. I love potatoes and cinnamon rolls; I'll eat a baked potato occasionally and maybe have a cinnamon roll three times a year.

*Cheryl Ladd*

# What's Your Poison?

Your grandmother's is the greatest place to hang out when you're young. It's the only place you can drink heavily without anyone noticing.

*Rhona Cameron*

It's OK for old people to drink heavily at night, because they can go up to bed on the electric chair thing attached to the staircase.

*Rhona Cameron*

I like my whisky old and my women young.

*Errol Flynn*

# What's Your Poison?

If more people did WI, there'd be half the need for hallucinogenic drugs.

*Chris,* Calendar Girls

I can't say to myself, "I haven't had a drink in 15 years; I could have a glass of champagne and be OK." That might be true, but history says when I opened that bottle of champagne, I sat there and drank it until it was gone.

*Samuel L Jackson*

I have to confess that I always enjoyed smoking – two fags and a cup of coffee got bowels and brain going in the mornings.

*Bryan Forbes*

I mean, I look all right. I could look a lot worse, considering what I've tipped down my throat over the course of the decades.

*Paul Weller*

When I'm watching *Coronation Street* and Rita goes into the Rovers Return for her gin and tonic or whatever, then I'll crack open a bottle of champagne. That's the only way to watch it.

*Cilla Black*

Smoking helped steady the nerves during two world wars.

*Winnie Langley, aged 100 despite having smoked for 93 years*

# What's Your Poison?

"What do I look like? Are you a fool?"

*Mr Tony Ralls, 72-year-old grandfather of three on being asked by staff at a Morrison's supermarket to prove he was over 21 before being allowed to purchase alcohol*

I simply lost the plot after discovering that by misusing prescription drugs, and washing them down with a few glasses of cheap wine, I could blot out reality.

*Tony Blackburn*

I like it not to be too large. I have small hands and a small head, and I don't want a cigar that's bigger than both of those parts of my body.

*Demi Moore*

I have smoked ever since infant school and I have never thought about quitting. There were not all the health warnings like there are today when I started. It was the done thing.

*Winnie Langley, speaking at her 100th birthday party*

I like red wine because it's more sophisticated, more complex and mature. It's a bit like me, no longer young but not old yet either.

*Mick Hucknall*

I like the odd glass of wine, a coffee and a cigarette. As you get older you can't see the wrinkles.

*Jerry Hall*

I used to be on about 40 a day, Lambert & Butler, full strength, lethal things. They had to lay off about 60 staff when I gave up, fucking awful.

*Paul O'Grady*

I'm very serious about no alcohol, no drugs. Life is too beautiful.

*Jim Carrey*

As is the case with most addicts, I thought I could handle it, that I could control it. I really had no idea that I would in fact become a slave.

*Marianne Faithful*

People always say I shouldn't be burning the candle at both ends, maybe because they don't have a big enough candle.

*George Best*

# Growing Old Disgracefully

I'm not sure what to think of the Rolling Stones. They seem to have gone so far past their use-by date that it really doesn't matter any more.

*Anon*

I got news for you. We're still a bunch of tough bastards. String us up and we still won't die.

*Keith Richards*

# Growing Old Disgracefully

When I was young, the old regarded me as an outrageous young fellow, and now that I'm old the young regard me as an outrageous old fellow.

*Fred Hoyle*

I hope there's a tinge of disgrace about me. Hopefully, there's one good scandal left in me yet.

*Diana Rigg*

The British press have been giving me six months to live for 20 years. They must be getting pissed off.

*Shane MacGowan*

I like growing old because it makes me feel like I'm not a wanker any more.

*Anon*

I'll be the 70-year-old in the tie-dye T-shirt taking Ecstasy in the night-club, being wheeled out in a trolley.

*Rupert Everett*

I hope to age disgracefully; it's the baby boomer mentality. Our generation is really determined not to grow old.

*Lulu*

While some of her fans will welcome another chance to see Cilla Black's shapely pins, others will be wondering whether a woman on the verge of her bus pass should be showing a little more decorum.

The Daily Mail

The older I get, the less I care about making a fool of myself.

*Mariella Frostrup*

## The Meaning of Life

Life may have no meaning. Or even worse, it may have a meaning of which I disapprove.

*Ashleigh Brilliant*

We think things end, but really life continues to reinvent itself.

*Olympia Dukakis*

Life is what it is and it gives you what it does. You have to make the best of it.

*Simone Urdl*

You know what my philosophy of life is? That it's important to have some laughs, but you got to suffer a little too, because otherwise you miss the whole point.

*Woody Allen,* Broadway Danny Rose

Life rarely gives us what we want at the moment we consider appropriate. Adventures do occur, but not punctually.

*Peggy Ashcroft,* Passage to India

# The Meaning of Life

The question is – have I learned anything about life? Only that human beings are divided into mind and body. The mind embraces all the nobler aspirations, like poetry and philosophy, but the body has all the fun.

*Woody Allen,* Love and Death

I finally figured out the only reason to be alive is to enjoy it.

*Rita Mae Brown*

You fall out of your mother's womb, you crawl across open country under fire and drop into your grave.

*Quentin Crisp*

How much do you engage yourself in what's truly real and important in life? That's the individual question.

*Ted Danson*

Here is the test to find whether your mission on Earth is finished: if you're alive, it isn't.

*Richard Bach*

We're all getting older. I celebrate life. We are far too concerned in present day society in measuring life in years. It's got bugger all to do with years, it's what you do in them.

*Roger Daltrey*

I used to trouble about what life was for – now being alive seems sufficient reason.

*Joanna Field*

Mere longevity is a good thing for those who watch life from the side lines. For those who play the game, an hour may be a year, a single day's work an achievement for eternity.

*Helen Hayes*

I think I've discovered the secret of life – you just hang around until you get used to it.

*Charles Schulz*

We all start off as sperm and end up as ash; our life amounts to jacking off into an ashtray.

*Sean Hughes*

# The Benefit of My Wisdom

The way I see it, if you want the rainbow, you gotta put up with the rain.

*Dolly Parton*

Get busy living, or get busy dying.

The Shawshank Redemption

Don't be so humble – you are not that great.

*Golda Meir, to a visiting diplomat*

It is a good rule in life never to apologise. The right sort of people do not want apologies and the wrong sort take a mean advantage of them.

*P G Wodehouse*

# The Benefit of My Wisdom

In my youth I stressed freedom and in my old age I stress order. I have made the great discovery that liberty is a product of order.

*Will Durant*

The best angle for looking through bi-focals is when you lean way back and look through the lens bottoms, thus affording the public a spectacular panoramic view of your nasal passages.

*Dave Barry*

Be yourself, be pleasant, play hard and have no regrets.

*Jimmy Buffett*

Have regular hours for work and play; make each day both useful and pleasant; and prove that you understand the worth of time by employing it well. Then youth will be delightful, old age will bring few regrets and life will become a beautiful success.

*Louisa May Alcott*

I don't believe in pessimism. If something doesn't come up the way you want, forge ahead. If you think it's going to rain, it will.

*Clint Eastwood*

I've learnt that you're defined by what you say no to. If you say yes to everything, there's bound to be disappointment in your life.

*Lenny Henry*

# The Benefit of My Wisdom

The average person thinks he isn't.

*Father Larry Lorenzoni*

You got to be careful if you don't know where you're going, because you might not get there.

*Yogi Berra*

'Tis better to be silent and be thought a fool, than to speak and remove all doubt.

*Mark Twain*

Sometimes you have to make a decision to be happy.

*Olympia Dukakis*

You have to remind yourself that it is only one ride, isn't it?

*Elaine Paige*

If you don't learn to laugh at troubles, you won't have anything to laugh at when you grow old.

*Edgar Watson Howe*

There is a trade off – as you grow older you gain wisdom, but you lose spontaneity.

*Kenny Rogers*

If you don't want to get old, kill yourself while you're young. Yiddish Proverb. (Actually, that's a bit drastic. I know a wonderful plastic surgeon.)

*Adrienne E Gusoff*

# The Benefit of My Wisdom

Don't stay in bed, unless you can make money in bed.

*George Burns*

Cherish all your happy moments; they make a fine cushion for old age.

*Booth Tarkington*

Develop your eccentricities while you are young. That way, when you get old, people won't think you're going gaga.

*David Ogilvy*

It's better to burn out than to fade away.

*Neil Young*

In the end you can only be yourself. You have to stumble on in your own way.

*Helen Mirren*

All of life is a coming home. Salesmen, secretaries, coal miners, beekeepers, sword swallowers, all of us. All the restless hearts of the world, all trying to find a way home.
*Robin Williams,* Patch Adams

In a relationship, it is better to be the leaver than the leavee.

*Woody Allen,* Everyone Says I Love You

You better know what you want to do before someone knows it for you.

*Billy Bob Thornton,* The Astronaut Farmer

# The Benefit of My Wisdom

A man that doesn't spend time with his family can never be a real man.

*Marlon Brando,* The Godfather

We live all too brief a span. What little we have should not be wasted.

*Richard Burton,* Anne of a Thousand Days

Which would you rather have, what's behind or what might be ahead?

*Montgomery Clift,* Red River

A good plan today is better than a perfect plan tomorrow.

*Robert De Niro,* Wag the Dog

All I know is the choices you make dictate the life you lead. "To thine own self be true."

*Danny De Vito,* Renaissance Man

But you can't stop and think… too much, because you'd never get going then. You have to find something and do it. If you start intellectualising, you're going to be very unhappy.

*Terry Wogan*

The thing women have got to learn is that nobody gives you power. You just take it.

*Roseanne Barr*

Always be a little kinder than necessary.

*James M Barrie*

# The Benefit of My Wisdom

The fact is, it seems, that the most you can hope is to be a little less, in the end, the creature you were in the beginning and the middle.

*Samuel Beckett*

You have to know how to accept rejection and reject acceptance.

*Ray Bradbury*

It takes courage to grow up and become who you really are.

*ee cummings*

If you really want to make a difference, the challenge can be onerous.

*Baroness Valerie Amos*

You don't have to be rich and famous. You just have to be an ordinary person, doing extraordinary things.

*Joan Armatrading*

Ever tried? Ever failed? No matter. Try again. Fail again. Fail better.

*Samuel Beckett*

Be a streak of red against the gray. Do it young, don't let time slip away.

*Bob Geldof*

My philosophy now isn't to live happily, but hopefully ever after.

*Paul O'Grady*

# The Benefit of My Wisdom

Only two things are infinite – the universe and human stupidity, and I'm not so sure about the universe.

*Stephen Fry*

The knowledge that every action has a consequence kept me from making a complete and utter arse of myself. I hope.

*Toyah Wilcox*

To know how to grow old is the master-work of wisdom and one of the most difficult chapters in the great art of living.

*Henri Frederic Amiel*

Advice in old age is foolish; for what can be more absurd than to increase our provisions for the road the nearer we approach to our journey's end.

*Marcus Tullius Cicero*

If it has tyres and testicles, you're going to have trouble with it… and I think that sums it up.

*Kim Cattrall*

For the world to be interesting, you have to be manipulating it all the time.

*Brian Eno*

Never comment on a woman's rear end. Never use the words "large" or "size" with "rear end". Never. Avoid the area altogether. Trust me.

*Tim Allen*

# The Benefit of My Wisdom

Never trust a man, who when left alone with a tea cosy… Doesn't try it on.

*Billy Connolly*

Turn up your radio. Watch lots of telly and eat loads of choc. Feel guilty. Stay up all night. Learn everything in six hours that has taken you two years to compile. That's how I did it.

*Dawn French*

Yesterday is history, tomorrow is a mystery, today is God's gift, that's why we call it the present.

*Joan Rivers*

It's the responsibility of everyone to figure their shit out.

*Sandra Bernhard*

Anyone can be beautiful, land a rock-star boyfriend and get hooked on drugs. What's important is to be a human being, to learn how to live with yourself.

*Marianne Faithful*

Remember that every life is a special problem, which is not yours but another's; and content yourself with the terrible algebra of your own.

*Henry James*

It is my invariable custom to say something flattering to begin with so that I shall be excused if by any chance I put my foot in it later on.

*Prince Philip*

If you're 48 and you haven't seen people in 30 years, don't do it. They're 48. They look like parents.

*Bill Cosby*

## Experience Comes With Age

Experience is a great advantage. The problem is that when you get the experience, you're too damned old to do anything about it.

*Jimmy Connors*

A proof that experience is of no use, is that the end of one love does not prevent us from beginning another.

*Paul Bourget*

You take all of the experience and judgment of men over 50 out of the world and there wouldn't be enough left to run it.

*Henry Ford*

With age comes experience and with experience comes judgement.

*Sir Menzies Campbell*

Human beings, who are almost unique in having the ability to learn from the experience of others, are also remarkable for their apparent disinclination to do so.

*Douglas Adams*

# Losing It!

Experience is that marvellous thing that enables you to recognise a mistake when you make it again.

*F P Jones*

# Losing It!

Old minds are like old horses; you must exercise them if you wish to keep them in working order.

*John Quincy Adams*

The young have aspirations that never come to pass, the old have reminiscences of what never happened.

*Saki*

It is hard enough to remember my opinions, without also remembering my reasons for them!

*Friedrich Nietzsche*

I have the worst memory ever so no matter who comes up to me – they're just, like, "I can't believe you don't remember me!" I'm like, "Oh Dad I'm sorry!"

*Ellen DeGeneres*

If you're trying to remember a happy memory, don't think back to a time when you were ALSO thinking of a happy memory, because man, how long does this go on?

*Jack Handey*

# Losing It!

If you want to test your memory, try to recall what you were worrying about one year ago today.

*E Joseph Cossman*

The advantage of a bad memory is that one enjoys several times the same good things for the first time.

*Friedrich Nietzsche*

Happiness is good health and a bad memory.

*Ingrid Bergman*

Memory is like an orgasm. It's a lot better if you don't have to fake it.

*Cray Seymore*

Recollection is the only paradise from which we cannot be turned out.

*Jean Paul Richter*

God gave us memory so that we might have roses in December.

*James M Barrie*

One of the keys to happiness is a bad memory.

*Rita Mae Brown*

Old age is remembering Cup Final teams and goals of generations past far more vividly than you can those of, well, only two days ago.

*Frank Keating*

# Losing It!

My husband complained to me, he said "I can't even remember when we last had sex," and I said, "Well I can and that's why we ain't doin' it."

*Roseanne Barr*

People will remember you better if you always wear the same outfit.

*David Byrne*

When I was younger, I could remember anything, whether it happened or not.

*Mark Twain*

I never heard of an old man forgetting where he had buried his money! Old people remember what interests them: the dates fixed for their lawsuits, and the names of their debtors and creditors.

*Marcus Tullius Cicero*

How is it that our memory is good enough to retain the least triviality that happens to us, and yet not good enough to recollect how often we have told it to the same person.

*Duc de la Rochefoucauld*

Interestingly, according to modern astronomers, space is infinite. This is a very comforting thought – particularly for people who can never remember where they have left things.

*Woody Allen*

## The Past

I find that the further I go back, the better things were, whether they happened or not.

*Mark Twain*

Events in the past may be roughly divided into those which probably never happened and those which do not matter.

*William Ralph Inge*

I've got my faults, but living in the past isn't one of them. There's no future in it.

*Sparky Anderson*

I tend to live in the past, because most of my life is there.

*Herb Caen*

Things happen more frequently in the future than they do in the past.

*Booth Gardener*

The past always looks better than it was; it's only pleasant because it isn't here.

*Finley Peter Dunne*

I don't live in the past at all; I'm always wanting to do something new. I make a point of constantly trying to forget and get things out of my mind.

*Brian Eno*

We need not destroy the past. It is gone.

*John Cage*

# Things They Wish They'd Never Said

There is no reason anyone would want a computer in their home.

*Ken Olson, president, chairman and founder of Digital Equipment Corporation, 1977*

We don't like their sound, and guitar music is on the way out.

*Decca Recording Company, rejecting the Beatles, in 1962*

Who the hell wants to hear actors talk?

*Harry Morris Warner (1881-1958), co-founder of Warner Brothers, in 1927*

The concept is interesting and well-formed, but in order to earn better than a 'C', the idea must be feasible.

*A Yale University management professor, in response to student Fred Smith's paper proposing reliable overnight delivery service (Smith went on to found Federal Express)*

I think there is a world market for maybe five computers.

*Thomas Watson (1874-1956), Chairman of IBM, in 1943*

# Things They Wish They'd Never Said

Colour television! Bah, I won't believe it until I see it in black and white.

*Samuel Goldwyn*

I don't normally do requests, unless I'm asked to.

*Richard Whiteley*

Red squirrels... you don't see many of them since they became extinct.

*Michael Aspel, Radio 2*

Did you write the words or the lyrics?

*Bruce Forsyth*

So Carol, you're a housewife and mother. And have you got any children?

*Michael Barrymore*

For NASA, space is still a high priority.

*Dan Quayle*

It was completely quiet in the stadium – but noisy.

*John Humphreys*

And we journalists are taught to avoid clichés like the plague.

*Barry Norman*

If history repeats itself, I should think we can expect the same thing again.

*Terry Venables*

# Things They Wish They'd Never Said

My fellow Americans, I am pleased to tell you I just signed legislation which outlaws Russia forever. The bombing will begin in five minutes.

*Ronald Reagan, during a radio microphone test*

And don't forget – on Sunday you can hear the two-minute silence on Radio 1.

*Steve Wright*

I must declare an interest in this and say that I know absolutely nothing at all about guns.

*Jimmy Young*

We spend weeks and hours every day preparing the Budget.

*Ronald Reagan*

We are now living in the age in which we live.

*Ann Burdis*

If we can just get young people to do the same as their fathers did, that is, wear condoms.

*Richard Branson*

Nigel and I hit it off like a horse on fire.

*Tony Britton*

Marble Arch was outside the Palace, but now Marble Arch is at Marble Arch.

*David Dimbleby*

# Things They Wish They'd Never Said

If it weren't for electricity we'd all be watching television by candlelight.

*George Gobol*

I have opinions of my own – strong opinions – but I don't always agree with them.

*George Bush*

We all know the leopard can't change his stripes.

*Al Gore*

I have lost friends, some by death, others through sheer inability to cross the street.

*Virginia Woolf*

Ah! Isn't that nice, the wife of the Cambridge president is kissing the cox of the Oxford crew.

*Harry Carpenter*

We now have exactly the same situation as we had at the start of the race, only exactly the opposite.

*Murray Walker*

There's no question that the minute I got elected, the storm clouds on the horizon were getting nearly directly overhead.

*George Bush*

If you can't stand the heat in the dressing-room, get out of the kitchen.

*Terry Venables*

# Things They Wish They'd Never Said

Fred Davis, the doyen of snooker, now 67 years of age and too old to get his leg over, prefers to use his left hand.

*Ted Lowe, snooker commentator*

This is really a lovely horse, I once rode her mother.

*Ted Walsh (horse racing commentator)*

Jimmy Hill: "Don't sit on the fence Terry, what chance do you think Germany has got of getting through?"
Terry Venables: "I think it's 50–50."

I think we agree the past is over.

*George Bush*

Certain people are for me and certain people are pro me.

*Terry Venables*

What makes this game so delightful is that when both teams get the ball they are attacking their opponents' goal.

*Jimmy Hill*

He's very fast and if he gets a yard ahead of himself nobody will catch him.

*Bobby Robson*

I've got a gut feeling in my stomach.

*Alan Sugar*

# Things They Wish They'd Never Said

What will you do when you leave football, Jack – will you stay in football?

*Stuart Hall*

I have made good judgments in the past. I have made good judgments in the future.

*George Bush*

We are ready for any unforeseen event that may or may not occur.

*Dan Quayle*

This administration is doing everything we can to end the stalemate in an efficient way. We're making the right decisions to bring the solution to an end.

*George Bush*

We're trying to get unemployment to go up and I think we're going to succeed.

*Ronald Reagan*

Reports that say that something hasn't happened are always interesting to me, because as we know, there are known knowns; there are things we know we know. We also know there are known unknowns; that is to say, we know there are some things we do not know. But there are also unknown unknowns – the ones we don't know we don't know.

*Donald Rumsfeld*

We don't want to go back to tomorrow, we want to go forward.

*Dan Quayle*

## Regrets

If I had to do my life over, I would change every single thing I have done.

*Ray Davies*

It's the things I might have said that fester.

*Clemence Dane*

Regret for the things we did can be tempered by time; it is regret for the things we did not do that is inconsolable.

*Sydney J Harris*

Regret for wasted time is more wasted time.

*Mason Cooley*

## I'm Too Old To Have To Put Up With...

Those lavatory doors which open inwards in such a way you have to back up on to the seat to get out. Golfing stories. Marzipan.

*Denis Norden*

Wire coat-hangers.

*Lawrence Olivier*

People who carry golfing umbrellas the size of Croydon.
It's only a bit of rain, not a monsoon. They nearly have
me eye out.

*Paul O'Grady*

Cold coffee, lukewarm champagne and overexcited
women.

*Orson Welles*

Living with, or even visiting, one whose feelings differ
widely from your own with regard to the admission of
fresh air.

*James Anderson*

## Critical Old Codgers

As one gets older and body maintenance becomes a
constant necessity, I find that one of the few
compensations is to be able to indulge in a good old
whinge with friends.

*Bryan Forbes*

It seems to be a lad or ladette culture in which the opium
of the people is football, everything is aimed at the lowest
common denominator and the music is aimed at an age
group somewhere between ten and maximum 20.
They're aiming it at the groin.

*Terry Wogan*

# Critical Old Codgers

The English like eccentrics. They just don't like them living next door.

*Julian Clary*

I don't think I'm qualified to answer [whether I'm a generous person]. If a friend needed something, I'd gladly buy it. On the other hand, £1.75 for an espresso? Preposterous.

*Tom Conti*

But it seems to me that we long ago moved from an environment in which litter was a local problem. We are no longer a green and pleasant land spotted with filthy places. We are a filthy island in which there is now an occasional oasis of cleanliness.

*Jeremy Paxman*

Yeah, I like football. Yeah, I talk the way I do. But that don't mean I'm a lad. What you do ain't who you are. I don't even go out very much, as it 'appens. I can't see the point in poncing about down the Groucho.

*Danny Baker*

I wish people would take more notice of rubbish. It's so unnecessary. I wish people wouldn't chuck rubbish out of their cars.

*Joan Armatrading*

I hate lads and the whole laddish movement. It's one-dimensional, innit? It's oafish and it ain't me.

*Danny Baker*

# Critical Old Codgers

I'm amazed by how compliant people are in this country. They go into service stations – "cathedrals of despair", as I call them – where baseball-capped ghouls of the night lord it over their congealed bean kingdoms, their fried-bread twilights, their neon demi-mondes, tempting you to become them, undead. "Ooh, beans on toast, £18.95, very reasonable… "

*Bill Bailey*

I'm definitely in favour of raising the minimum driving age. In fact, I think it should be raised every year, to keep my son from ever reaching it. I think that when my son is 58 years old and comes to visit me in the old person's home, he should arrive via skateboard.

*Dave Barry*

What language are you talking in now? It appears to be Bollocks.

*Richard Wilson*

California is like an artificial limb the rest of the country doesn't really need. You can quote me on that.

*Saul Bellow*

I'd move to Los Angeles if New Zealand and Australia were swallowed up by a tidal wave, if there was a bubonic plague in England and if the continent of Africa disappeared from some Martian attack.

*Russell Crowe*

# Critical Old Codgers

When you look at Prince Charles, don't you think that someone in the royal family knew someone in the royal family?

*Robin Williams*

Thou shall not kill. Thou shall not commit adultery. Don't eat pork. I'm sorry, what was that last one? Don't eat pork. God has spoken. Is that the word of God or is that pigs trying to outsmart everybody?

*Jon Stewart*

Pensioners are by far the worst drivers. They are spiteful, dithering, old and in the way. They should have their licences taken away.

*Jeremy Clarkson*

Where lipstick is concerned, the important thing is not colour, but to accept God's final word on where your lips end.

*Jerry Seinfeld*

The freedom that women were supposed to have found in the '60s largely boiled down to easy contraception and abortion; things to make life easier for men in fact.

*Julie Burchill*

The world falls into two halves – those who worship Ruby Wax and those who get out of the bath to pee.

*A A Gill*

I don't laugh out loud, hardly ever. Maybe once every five years.

*Rowan Atkinson*

# Whatever Happened to the Good Old Days?

What good old days?

*Rose Butt, aged 93*

Patsy: Who dies in their own vomit these days?
Eddy: Nobody!

Absolutely Fabulous

Now there's nothing you don't know about people. You can find out everything about everybody and I think that's a rather eroding thing. I would be put right off if I was coming into the profession now. I wouldn't like it at all.

*Judi Dench*

The older I get the better I used to be.

*Lee Trevino*

I played in a lovely era, much more guile and finesse, longer rallies, drop shots, wooden rackets, balls straight out of the box.

*Sue Barker*

# Forty Winks

In the good old days… you were poor… you got ill… and you died!

*Rik Mayall as Alan B'Stard in* The New Statesman

I've never understood why people consider youth a time of freedom and joy. It's probably because they have forgotten their own.

*Margaret Atwood*

In my youth there were words you couldn't say in front of a girl; now you can't say "girl".

*Tom Lehrer*

When I was a kid they were trying to sell me spot medicine. Now they're trying to sell girls $400 shoes and $800 handbags, and I just think to myself, "This is crazy."

*Kim Cattrall*

In my day, I would only have sex with a man if I found him extremely attractive. These days girls seem to choose them in much the same way as they might choose to suck on a boiled sweet.

*Mary Wesley*

# Forty Winks

Consciousness: that annoying time between naps.

*Anon*

Old women snore violently. They are like bodies
into which bizarre animals have crept at night; the
animals are vicious, bawdy, noisy. How they snore!
There is no shame to their snoring. Old women turn
into old men.

*Joyce Carol Oates*

I never drink coffee at lunch. I find it keeps me awake
for the afternoon.

*Ronald Reagan*

Cherie has many excellent qualities, but once she
goes to sleep, it takes a minor nuclear explosion to
wake her up.

*Tony Blair*

Naps are nature's way of reminding you that life is nice
– like a beautiful, softly swinging hammock strung
between birth and infinity.

*Peggy Noonan*

It's amazing when you get to a certain age and you
talk about sleep in the same way you spoke about
getting inebriated… I got eight hours last night. It
was fantastic!

*Johnny Depp*

Life is something to do when you can't get to sleep.

*Fran Lebowitz*

## One Hundred Years Plus

I honestly think farm living is responsible for her longevity. There wasn't a lot of time for indulgence – it was all work, work, work.

> *Kirk Curnutt, great-grandson of Edna Parker, who at*
> *age 114 is the world's oldest living person.*

At her 120th birthday party, when Jeanne Calment was asked by a young journalist, "Will I see you at next year's birthday party?" She instantly shot back, "I don't see why not; you look pretty healthy to me!"

> *Jeanne Calment*

One of my favourite life stories was about a 106–year-old man, Ken Batchelder, who wrote his autobiography in his '80s, then had to update it and write part II at age 94 after he visited Russia and China on a nuclear powered icebreaker…

> *Amy Silvers*

We don't get to choose our parents, but we select our lifestyles.

> *R Waldo McBurney, 104-year-old beekeeper*
> *and fitness advocate*

No one tries the patience of his relatives like a rich centenarian.

> *Anon*

Cats are my favorite animal. We have eight here and caring for them gives me determination to carry on.

*Father Nicolas Kao Se Tsien, a 109-year-old Trappist monk*

I never damaged my body with liquor.

*Emiliano Mercado de Toro, aged 115, who quit a 76-year smoking habit when he was 90*

He lived a great life. Obviously, he was well put together. He smoked cigars, drank beer and ate greasy food. He was an amazing man.

*Lisa Saxton, great-granddaughter of John McMorran, who died aged 113*

Another way to live to be 100 is to reach 99 and then live very carefully.

*Anon*

I figure if George Burns can smoke 20 cigars a day his whole life and live to be 100, why should I worry if they're bad for me?

*Milton Berle*

I don't know. It comes and goes. And it's been coming and going for so long – I don't find it funny.

*Isabella Gibson on her 99th birthday, when asked for the secret of her longevity*

Once you've lived as long as me, only then can you tell me not to smoke.

*Jeanne Calment at age 118, talking to her doctor*

# One Hundred Years Plus

I've been forgotten by a good God.

*Jeanne Calment on her 120th birthday*

One should eat a hearty meal before going to sleep and say "thank you" to everybody.

*A recipe for longevity from Japan's oldest woman,*
*Ione Minagawa, aged 113*

I'd like to do a bit of travelling. I'd like to go to places like Egypt and China. Places like that.

*Muriel, aged 105*

Attitude is 90% and circumstances are 10%. And you have to clean your teeth three times a day.

*Marge, aged 102, when asked the secret of her longevity*

I don't know why they make such a fuss about a man of a certain age, like me, working. If you want to work and carry on instead of getting a grumpy old git. There you are. If I couldn't keep going I'd rather snuff it.

*Buster, aged 100, Britain's oldest working man*

You want me to just sit and do nothing?

*Marge, aged 102, when asked why she still walks a mile every*
*day and works out with weights*

Life begins at 80, gets better when you reach 90. But ooh when you reach 100…!

*"Rosie", aged 101*

That's why I've lived so long. I haven't had the worry of a husband.

*Gracie, aged 105*

He doesn't want me up there.

*Charlotte, aged 110*

It's a bit of a tragedy, age… isn't it?

*Sydney, aged 102*

# The Secrets of Longevity

If you ask what is the single most important key to longevity, I would have to say it is avoiding worry, stress and tension. And if you didn't ask me, I'd still have to say it.

*George Burns*

Hangin' in.

*Elizabeth Taylor*

If you live long, with intensity, you see all kinds of interesting things. It's stupid to die before you're 80. I lived longer than Bob Hope!

*May Ushiyama, 94-year-old head of the Hollywood Beauty Salon in Tokyo*

You can't reach old age by another man's road. My habits protect my life, but they would assassinate you.

*Mark Twain*

# The Secrets of Longevity

Look alive. Here comes a buzzard.

*Lady Stella Reading*

At the end of the world there will be cockroaches,
Keith Richards and Ozzy Osbourne.

*Sharon Osbourne*

If all else fails, immortality can always be assured by
spectacular error.

*John Kenneth Galbraith*

Immortality is the genius to move others long after you
yourself have stopped moving.

*Frank Rooney*

A wife is essential to great longevity; she is the
receptacle of half a man's cares and two-thirds of his
ill-humor.

*Charles Reade*

How do you live a long life? Take a two-mile walk
every morning before breakfast.

*Harry S Truman*

The quality, not the longevity, of one's life is what is
important.

*Martin Luther King Jr*

I always liked to exercise when I was young – walk,
swim and cycle – and now I try to keep going as much
as I can. I exercise to music once a week and I don't sit

down to be waited on. I still do a few jobs. I knit a lot for a charity and I still read the papers.

*Winifred Timbrell, aged 92*

I don't know why I've lived so long, maybe it's just that I've done everything in moderation – drinking, walking, cycling and a lot of my life has been outdoors.

*Duncan Clark, aged 92*

The secret of longevity is genes. I've been lucky enough not to inherit any weaknesses, but I've also been sensible. I've never smoked and I've always believed in super foods and that.

*Liz Smith*

# As Fit as a Fiddle

HEALTH

I saw a specialist who asked me: "Are you familiar with the phrase faecal impaction?" I said: "I think I saw that one with Glenn Close and Michael Douglas."

*Bob Monkhouse*

I wouldn't say I'm fanatically health conscious, but my mother suffered from osteoporosis which made her virtually housebound, so I do weight-lifting to strengthen my bones.

*Victoria Wood*

# As Fit as a Fiddle

One finger in the throat and one in the rectum makes a good diagnostician.

*William Osler*

Pain was something we were expected to endure. But I doubt very much if you would be entirely happy today if a doctor threw a towel in your face and jumped on you with a knife.

*Roald Dahl*

The chief danger in life is that you may take too many precautions.

*Alfred Adler*

I don't know why it is we are in such a hurry to get up when we fall down. You might think we would lie there and rest for a while.

*Max Eastman*

Hospital rooms seem to have vastly more ceiling than any rooms people live in.

*Bertha Damon*

In hospitals there is no time off for good behavior.

*Josephine Tey*

A trip to the hospital is always a descent into the macabre. I have never trusted a place with shiny floors.

*Terry Tempest Williams*

Our body is a well-set clock, which keeps good time, but if it be too much or indiscreetly tampered with, the alarm runs out before the hour.

*Joseph Hall*

## Golden Ghettos

These days everybody lives to be 180 so we lock old people up – all those years of knowledge and experience – in retirement homes and instead listen to teenagers philosophizing on *Home and Away*.

*Anon*

If you associate enough with older people who do enjoy their lives, who are not stored away in any golden ghettos, you will gain a sense of continuity and of the possibility for a full life.

*Margaret Mead*

I have been very lonely in my life… which is why I decided to live with other people around. But don't call it a retirement home… "Retirement" implies "oldie" and all that and they don't like it.

*Liz Smith*

I'd rather rot on my own floor than be found by a bunch of bingo players in a nursing home.

*Florence King*

# In the Name of the Father...

I was thinking about how people seem to read the Bible
a whole lot more as they get older; then it dawned on
me... they're cramming for their final exam.

*George Carlin*

If it turns out that there is a God, I don't think that he's
evil. But the worst that you can say about him is that
basically he's an underachiever.

*Woody Allen*

I got nervous when I was asked to play God. We're both
around the same age, but we grew up in different
neighbourhoods.

*George Burns*

I know God will not give me anything I can't handle. I
just wish that He didn't trust me so much.

*Mother Teresa*

It is stupid of modern civilization to have given up
believing in the devil, when he is the only explanation
of it.

*Ronald Knox*

My own religious background is I'm a Protestant, a
Church of England Protestant. My father was a
Catholic, my mother was a Protestant, I was educated
by Jews and have a Muslim wife. So I'm very eclectic

about religion and I've met zealots of all of them. And there's always a slack madness about it.

*Michael Caine*

I believe in destiny. There must be a reason that I am as I am. There must be.

*Robin Williams*

To you, I'm an atheist. To God, I'm the loyal opposition.

*Woody Allen,* Stardust Memories

I'm a Jewish girl and I feel in a sense that that's very, very important in terms of relating, especially when you're too young to know where you come from and who you are, and what it is you stand for, and to have some spiritual connection. I have become a practicing Buddhist.

*Goldie Hawn*

I have a very close relationship with my Guardian Angel … When I really, really need strength and protection I visualise myself wrapped in my angel's wings and a furious light blasting outwards from us; this gives me the greatest surge of power I have ever experienced. For me it works.

*Toyah Wilcox*

If I were going to convert to any religion I would probably choose Catholicism, because it at least has female saints and the Virgin Mary.

*Margaret Atwood*

# Time Waits for No Man

Forgive, O Lord, my little jokes on thee and I'll forgive thy great big one on me.

*Robert Frost*

The deeper you get into yoga you realize it is a spiritual practice. It's a journey I'm making. I'm heading that way.

*Sting*

The bird tattooed rather badly on my left wrist is something I had done at about 18 years old by an old dyke from Naples... The swallow was supposed to enable my soul to leave my body sooner when I died, which was one of those crazy '60s theories.

*Marianne Faithful*

# Time Waits for No Man

I want to die slowly and nicely, in great surroundings, with my family. It is a bit shocking, isn't it?

*Dawn French*

I'd like to be remembered with a smile.

*June Whitfield*

When I die I want to decompose in a barrel of porter and have it served in all the pubs in Dublin.

*J P Donleavy*

# Time Waits for No Man

I was number one on the Who's Likely To Die list for ten years. I mean, I was really disappointed when I fell off the list.

*Keith Richards*

When you're getting older, you think about the things you can't do and all the reasons. But if I have to die in a hospital, I might as well die on Everest.

*Yuichiro Miura, planning another assent of Everest at 75*

I wouldn't mind being dead – it would be something new.

*Estelle Winwood, age 100*

A recent survey stated that the average person's greatest fear is having to give a speech in public. Somehow this ranked even higher than death, which was third on the list. So, you're telling me that at a funeral, most people would rather be the guy in the coffin than have to stand up and give a eulogy.

*Jerry Seinfield*

My uncle's dying wish – he wanted me on his lap.…
He was in the electric chair.

*Rodney Dangerfield*

I wouldn't mind being an old git in a massive house on the shores of Lake Geneva. Then I'd like to die suddenly and have millions of people weep at my televised funeral.

*Rupert Everett*

# Time Waits for No Man

Die

*Elliot Gould, when asked what project he has
always wanted to do*

You're a lot better looking in person.

*Harrison Ford, when asked "If heaven exists, what would
you want God to say to you at the Pearly Gates?"*

They say some people know when they're going to die.
My father definitely knew when he was going to die.
He shot himself you see.

*Alan Davies,* Auntie & Me

When I die, I'm leaving my body to science fiction.

*Steven Wright*

Guns are the best method for private suicide. Drugs are
too chancy. You might miscalculate and just have a good
time.

*P J O'Rourke*

Every year on the anniversary of Elvis's death we are
bombarded with Elvis films on TV and Elvis records on
the radio all day. How can we be assured the same thing
won't happen when Michael Ball dies?

*Mrs Merton*

# The Final Farewell .

FUNERALS

I wanna be cremated. Sprinkle my ashes with about two pounds of cocaine and snort me up… crying, "He sure makes a hulluva cut."

*Richard Pryor*

Amazing tradition. They throw a great party for you on the one day they know you can't come.

*Jeff Goldblum,* The Big Chill

If you want to really know what your friends and family think of you – die broke and then see who shows up for the funeral.

*Gregory Null*

I guess we're all thinking how sad it is that a man of such talent, of such capability for kindness, of such unusual intelligence, should now be spirited away at the age of only 48, before he'd… had enough fun. Well, I feel that I should say, "Nonsense! Good riddance to him, the free-loading bastard! I hope he's frying!" And the reason I feel I should say this is because he would never forgive me… if I threw away this glorious opportunity to shock you all on his behalf.

*John Cleese, reading a eulogy for Graham Chapman*

# The Last Word

The only two things we do with greater frequency when we get older is urinate and attend funerals.

*Anon*

To Harry Secombe: I hope you die first as I don't want you singing at my funeral.

*Spike Milligan*

Picasso was a delightful, kindly, friendly, simple little man. When I met him he was extremely excited and overjoyed that his mother-in-law had just died, and he was looking forward to the funeral.

*Edith Sitwell*

# The Last Word

Waiting are they? Well let 'em wait!

*General Mad Anthony Wayne when told by his doctors the angels were waiting for him*

I have spent my life laboriously doing nothing.

*James Abram Garfield*

Why fear death? It is the most beautiful adventure in life.

*Charles Frohman's last words before he sank in the wreck of the Lusitania*

Don't let it end like this. Tell them I said something.

*Francisco Villa*

Goodbye. I am leaving because I am bored.

*George Saunders*

Hovering between wife and death.

*James Montgomery, when asked how he was on his death bed*

This is no time for making new enemies.

*Voltaire, when asked on his deathbed to renounce Satan*

# Life After Death

After I die, I shall return to earth as a gatekeeper of a bordello and I won't let any of you – not a one of you – enter!

*Arturo Toscanini*

When you die, if you get a choice between going to regular heaven or pie heaven, choose pie heaven. It might be a trick, but if it's not, mmmmmmm, boy.

*Jack Handy*

Actually, I have only two things to worry about now: afterlife and reincarnation.

*Gail Parent*

These days, I spend a lot of time thinking about the hereafter. I go somewhere to get something… then wonder what I'm here after.

*Anon*

# Life After Death

I don't believe in the afterlife or ghosts, but something strange happened the other day. I went into Murphy's room and it was full of butterflies. A picture had also fallen off the wall. You have to wonder if he was trying to say something.

*Paul O'Grady, after the death of his partner*

I suspect that in another life I attended the Spanish Inquisition as a volunteer.

*Sandi Toksvig*

When you're dead, you're dead. That's it.

*Marlene Dietrich*

Geoff and I are twin souls. We believe we have met in a previous existence. Hypnotherapy sessions have led us to the astonishing conclusion that Geoff was Queen Victoria's chief lady-in-waiting and I was a porter employed by the Great Western Railway. It is this belief that keeps an undertow of physical excitement in our connubial union. Plus we are both fond of chips.

*Victoria Wood*

I am depressed because of the state of my life at the moment. I've got this 'orrible feeling that if there is such a thing as reincarnation, knowing my luck, I'll come back as me.

*Nicholas Lyndhurst as Rodney in* Only Fools and Horses

I'd like to believe in heaven, not least because I'd like to meet my mum and dad again. I'd like to know whether the Welsh dresser was meant to go to me or my brother, really.

*John Peel*

If there's a heaven for homosexuals it'll be very poorly lit and full of people they can be pretty confident they'll never meet again.

*Quentin Crisp*

If I were reincarnated, I would wish to be returned to earth as a killer virus to lower human population levels.

*Prince Philip*

# Index

# Index

# Index

# Index

# Index

# Index

# Index

# Index

# Index